Kaplan Publishing are constantly finding new ways to make a difference to yo... exciting online resources really ... different to students looking fo...

This book comes with free EN-gage online resources so that you can study anytime, anywhere.

Having purchased this book, you have access to the following online study materials:

CONTENT	ACCA (including FFA, FAB, FMA) Text	ACCA Kit	AAT Text	AAT Kit	FIA (excluding FFA, FAB, FMA) Text	FIA Kit
iPaper version of the book	✓	✓	✓	✓	✓	✓
Interactive electronic version of the book	✓					
Fixed tests / progress tests with instant answers	✓		✓			
Mock assessments online			✓	✓		
Material updates	✓	✓	✓	✓	✓	✓
Latest official ACCA exam questions		✓				
Extra question assistance using the signpost icon*		✓				
Timed questions with an online tutor debrief using the clock icon*		✓				
Interim assessment including questions and answers		✓				✓
Technical articles	✓	✓			✓	✓

* Excludes F1, F2, F3, FFA, FAB, FMA

How to access your online resources

Kaplan Financial students will already have a Kaplan EN-gage account and these extra resources will be available to you online. You do not need to register again, as this process was completed when you enrolled. If you are having problems accessing online materials, please ask your course administrator.

If you are already a registered Kaplan EN-gage user go to www.EN-gage.co.uk and log in. Select the 'add a book' feature and enter the ISBN number of this book and the unique pass key at the bottom of this card. Then click 'finished' or 'add another book'. You may add as many books as you have purchased from this screen.

If you purchased through Kaplan Flexible Learning or via the Kaplan Publishing website you will automatically receive an e-mail invitation to Kaplan EN·gage online. Please register your details using this email to gain access to your content. If you do not receive the e-mail or book content, please contact Kaplan Flexible Learning.

If you are a new Kaplan EN-gage user register at www.EN-gage.co.uk and click on the link contained in the email we sent you to activate your account. Then select the 'add a book' feature, enter the ISBN number of this book and the unique pass key at the bottom of this card. Then click 'finished' or 'add another book'.

Your Code and Information

This code can only be used once for the registration of one book online. This registration and your online content will expire when the final sittings for the examinations covered by this book have taken place. Please allow one hour from the time you submit your book details for us to process your request.

Please scratch the film to access your EN-gage code.

4qBe-Vuaq-Sbpn-JB4K

Please be aware that this code is case-sensitive and you will need to include the dashes within the passcode, but not when entering the ISBN. For further technical support, please visit www.EN-gage.co.uk

INTERMEDIATE LEVEL

MA2

Managing Costs and Finances

STUDY TEXT

British Library Cataloguing-in-Publication Data

A catalogue record for this book is available from the British Library.

Published by:
Kaplan Publishing UK
Unit 2 The Business Centre
Molly Millars Lane
Wokingham
RG41 2QZ

ISBN   978-0-85732-726-0

© Kaplan Financial Limited, 2012

Printed and bound in Great Britain

Acknowledgments

We are grateful to the Association of Chartered Certified Accountants for permission to reproduce past examination questions. The answers have been prepared by Kaplan Publishing.

All rights reserved. No part of this publication may be reproduced, stored in a retrieval system, or transmitted, in any form or by any means, electronic, mechanical, photocopying, recording or otherwise, without the prior written permission of Kaplan Publishing.

The text in this material and any others made available by any Kaplan Group company does not amount to advice on a particular matter and should not be taken as such. No reliance should be placed on the content as the basis for any investment or other decision or in connection with any advice given to third parties. Please consult your appropriate professional adviser as necessary. Kaplan Publishing Limited and all other Kaplan group companies expressly disclaim all liability to any person in respect of any losses or other claims, whether direct, indirect, incidental, consequential or otherwise arising in relation to the use of such materials.

CONTENTS

	Page
Introduction	v
Syllabus and study guide	vii
The examination	xiii
Study skills and revision guidance	xv
Mathematical tables	xvii

Chapter

		Page
1	Management information	1
2	Cost accounting systems	19
3	Cost classification and cost behaviour	41
4	Accounting for materials	59
5	Material inventory control	75
6	Accounting for labour	89
7	Accounting for other expenses	113
8	Absorption costing	125
9	Marginal costing and absorption costing	157
10	Job and batch costing	171
11	Process costing	183
12	Service costing	207
13	CVP analysis	217
14	Decision making	237
15	Discounted cash flow and capital expenditure appraisal	259
16	The nature of cash and cash flows	291
17	Cash management, investing and finance	303
18	Cash budgets	329
19	Spreadsheets	355
Answers to activities and end of chapter questions		393
Index		447

INTRODUCTION

This is the new edition of the FIA study text for MA 2 – *Managing Costs and Finances,* fully updated and revised according to the examiner's comments.

Tailored to fully cover the syllabus, this Study Text has been written specifically for FIA students. A clear and comprehensive style, numerous examples and highlighted key terms help you to acquire the information easily. Plenty of activities and self test questions enable you to practise what you have learnt.

At the end of most of the chapters you will find practice questions. These are exam-style questions and will give you a very good idea of the way you will be tested.

SYLLABUS AND STUDY GUIDE

Position of the paper in the overall syllabus

Knowledge of MA1, M*anagement Information*, at the introductory level is required before commencing study for MA2.

This paper provides the basic techniques required to enable candidates to develop knowledge and understanding of how to prepare, process and present basic cost information to support management in planning and decision making in a variety of business contexts.

Candidates will need a sound understanding of the methods and techniques introduced in this paper to ensure that they can take them further in subsequent papers. The methods introduced in this paper are revisited and extended in FMA, *Management Accounting*.

Syllabus

A   Management information   Chapters 1 to 3
1. Management information requirements
2. Cost accounting systems
3. Cost classification

B   Cost recording   Chapters 4 to 7
1. Accounting for materials
2. Accounting for labour
3. Accounting for other expenses

C   Costing techniques   Chapters 8 to 12
1. Absorption costing
2. Marginal costing
3. Job and batch costing
4. Process costing
5. Service costing

D   Decision making   Chapters 13 to 15
1. Cost-volume-profit analysis
2. Factors affecting short term decision making
3. Principles of discounted cash flow

E   Cash management   Chapters 16 to 18
1. Nature of cash and cash flow
2. Cash management
3. Cash budgets
4. Investing and financing

F   Spreadsheets   Chapter 19
1. Spreadsheet system overview
2. Using computer spreadsheets
3. Presenting information in spreadsheets

Study guide

A MANAGEMENT INFORMATION

1 Management information requirements — Chapter 1

(a) Discuss the purpose of management information: planning, control and decision making.[K]

(b) Describe the features of useful management Information.[K]

(c) Discuss the nature, source and importance of both financial and non-financial information for managers.[K]

(d) Describe management responsibilities for cost, profit and investment and their effect on management information and performance measurement.[k]

(e) Explain the role of information technology in management information.[K]

(f) Explain the role of the trainee accountant.[K]

(g) Identify suitable formats for the presentation of management information according to purpose.[S]

2 Cost accounting systems — Chapter 2

(a) Explain the relationship between the cost/management accounting system and the financial accounting/management information systems (including interlocking and integrated bookkeeping systems).[K]

(b) Describe the process of accounting for input costs and relating them to work done. [K]

(c) Identify the documentation required, and the flow of documentation, for different cost accounting transactions.[S]

(d) Explain and illustrate the use of codes in categorising and processing transactions(including sequential, hierarchical, block, faceted and mnemonic coding methods.[K]

(e) Explain and illustrate the concept of cost units.[S]

(f) Describe the different methods of costing final outputs and their appropriateness to different types of business organisation.[S]

(g) Describe methods of capturing, processing, storing and outputting cost and management accounting data by computer.[K]

3 Cost classification — Chapter 3

(a) Describe the variety of cost classifications used for different purposes in a cost accounting system, including by responsibility, function, direct/indirect, behaviour.[K]

(b) Explain and illustrate the nature of variable, fixed and mixed (semi-variable, stepped fixed) costs.[S]

(c) Use the high-low method to separate semi-variable costs.[S]

(d) Use variable, fixed and semi-variable costs in cost analysis.[S]

(e) Analyse the effect of changing activity levels on unit costs.[S]

B COST RECORDING

1 Accounting for materials — Chapter 4 and 5

(a) Describe the main types of material classification.[K]

(b) Describe the procedures and documentation required to ensure the correct authorisation, coding, analysis and recording of direct and indirect material costs.[K]

(c) Explain, illustrate and evaluate the FIFO, LIFO and periodic and cumulative weighted average methods used to price materials issued from inventory.[S]

(d) Describe and illustrate the accounting for material costs.[S]

(e) Calculate material input requirements, and control measures, where wastage occurs.[S]

(f) Describe the procedures required to monitor inventory and to minimise discrepancies and losses.[K]

- (g) Explain and illustrate the costs of holding inventory and of being without inventory.[S]
- (h) Explain, illustrate and evaluate inventory control levels (minimum, maximum, reorder).[S]
- (i) Calculate and interpret optimal order quantities.[S]
- (j) Discuss the relationship between the materials costing system and the inventory control system.[K]

2   Accounting for labour   Chapter 6

- (a) Explain, illustrate and evaluate labour remuneration methods.[S]
- (b) Describe the operation of a payroll accounting system.[K]
- (c) Distinguish between direct and indirect labour costs. .[K]
- (d) Describe the procedures and documentation required to ensure the correct coding, analysis and recording of direct and indirect labour.[K]
- (e) Describe and illustrate the accounting for labour costs.[S]
- (f) Explain the relationship between the labour costing system and the payroll accounting system.[K]
- (g) Explain the causes and costs of, and calculate, labour turnover.[S]
- (h) Describe and illustrate measures of labour efficiency and utilisation (efficiency, capacity utilisation, production volume and idle time ratios).[S]

3   Costing of other expenses   Chapter 7

- (a) Describe the nature of expenses by function.[K]
- (b) Describe the procedures and documentation required to ensure the correct authorisation, coding, analysis and recording of direct and indirect expenses.[K]
- (c) Describe and calculate capital and revenue expenditure and the relevant accounting treatment.[K]
- (d) Calculate and explain depreciation charges using straight-line, reducing balance, machine hour and product units methods.[S]
- (e) Explain the relationship between the expenses costing system and the expense accounting system.[K]

C   COSTING TECHNIQUES

1   Absorption costing   Chapter 8 and 9

- (a) Explain the rationale for absorption costing.[K]
- (b) Describe the nature of production and service cost centres and their significance for production overhead allocation, apportionment and absorption.[K]
- (c) Describe the process of allocating, apportioning and absorbing production overheads to establish product costs.[K]
- (d) Apportion overheads to cost centres using appropriate bases.[S]
- (e) Re-apportion service cost centre overheads to production cost centres using direct and step down methods.[S]
- (f) Justify, calculate and apply production cost centre overhead absorption rates using labour hour and machine hour methods.[S]
- (g) Explain the relative merits of actual and pre determined absorption rates.[K]
- (h) Describe and illustrate the accounting for production overhead costs, including the analysis and interpretation of over/under absorption.[S]
- (i) Describe and apply methods of attributing non-production overheads to cost units.[S]
- (j) Calculate product costs using the absorption costing method.[S]

2   Marginal costing   Chapter 9

- (a) Explain and illustrate the concept of contribution.[S]
- (b) Prepare profit statements using the marginal costing method.[S]

- (c) Prepare profit statements using the absorption costing method.[S]
- (d) Compare and contrast the use of absorption and marginal costing for period profit reporting and inventory valuation.[K]
- (e) Reconcile the profits reported by absorption and marginal costing.[S]
- (f) Explain the usefulness of profit and contribution information respectively.[K]

3 Job and batch costing   Chapter 10

- (a) Identify situations where the use of job or batch costing is appropriate.[K]
- (b) Discuss the control of costs in job and batch costing.[K]
- (c) Apply cost plus pricing in job costing.[S]

4 Process costing   Chapter 11

- (a) Identify situations where the use of process costing is appropriate.[K]
- (b) Explain and illustrate the nature of normal and abnormal losses/gains.[S]
- (c) Calculate unit costs where losses are separated into normal and abnormal.[S]
- (d) Prepare process accounts where losses are separated into normal and abnormal.[S]
- (e) Account for scrap and waste.[S]
- (f) Distinguish between joint products and by-products.[K]
- (g) Explain the accounting treatment of joint products and by-products at the point of separation.[K]
- (h) Apportion joint process costs using net realisable values and weight/volume of output respectively.[S]
- (i) Discuss the usefulness of product cost/profit data from a joint process.[K]
- (j) Evaluate the benefit of further processing.[S]

5 Service costing   Chapter 12

- (a) Describe the characteristics of service costing.[K]
- (b) Describe the practical problems relating to the costing of services.[K]
- (c) Identify situations (cost centres and industries) where the use of service costing is appropriate.[S]
- (d) Illustrate suitable cost units that may be used for a variety of services.[S]
- (e) Calculate service unit costs in a variety of situations.[S]

D DECISION MAKING

1 Cost / volume / profit analysis   Chapter 13

- (a) Calculate contribution per unit and the contribution/sales ratio.[S]
- (b) Explain the concept of break-even and margin of safety.[K]
- (c) Use contribution per unit and contribution/sales ratio to calculate break even point and margin of safety.[S]
- (d) Analyse the effect on break-even point and margin of safety of changes in selling price and costs.[S]
- (e) Use contribution per unit and contribution/sales ratio to calculate the sales required to achieve a target profit.[S]
- (f) Interpret break-even and profit/volume charts for a single product or business.[S]

2 Factors affecting short term decision-making   Chapter 14

- (a) Explain the importance of the limiting factor concept.[K]
- (b) Identify the limiting factor in given situations.[S]
- (c) Formulate and determine the optimal production solution when there is a single resource constraint.[S]

	(d)	Solve make/buy-in problems when there is a single resource constraint.[S]		(e)	Explain the importance of cash flow management and its impact on liquidity and company survival (note: calculation of ratios is not required) .[K]
	(e)	Explain the concept of relevant costs.[K]	2	**Cash Management**	**Chapter 17**
	(f)	Apply the concept of relevant costs in business decisions.[S]		(a)	Outline the basic treasury functions.[K]
3	**Principles of discounted cash flow Chapter 16**			(b)	Describe cash handling procedures.[K]
	(a)	Explain and illustrate the difference between simple and compound interest, and between nominal and effective interest rates.[S]		(c)	Outline guidelines and legislation in relation to the management of cash balances in public sector organisations.[K]
	(b)	Explain and illustrate compounding and discounting.[S]		(d)	Describe how trends in the economic and financial environment can affect management of cash balances.[K]
	(c)	Explain the distinction between cash flow and profit and the relevance of cash flow to capital investment appraisal.[K]	3	**Cash budgets**	**Chapter 18**
	(d)	Explain and illustrate the net present value (NPV) and internal rate of return (IRR) methods of discounted cash flow.[S]		(a)	Explain the objectives of cash budgeting.[K]
				(b)	Explain and illustrate statistical techniques used in cash forecasting including moving averages and allowance for inflation.[S]
	(e)	Calculate present value using annuity and perpetuity formulae.[S]			
	(f)	Calculate payback (discounted and non-discounted).[S]		(c)	Prepare a cash budget/forecast .[S]
	(g)	Interpret the results of NPV, IRR and payback calculations of investment viability.[S]		(d)	Explain and illustrate how a cash budget can be used as a mechanism for monitoring and control.[S]
E	**CASH MANAGEMENT**		4	**Investing and financing**	**Chapter 17**
1	**Nature of cash and cash flow**	**Chapter 16**		(a)	Explain how surplus cash and cash deficit may arise.[K]
	(a)	Define cash and cash flow .[K]		(b)	Explain the following types of short term investments and the associated risks/returns.[K]:
	(b)	Outline the various sources of cash receipts and payments (including regular/exceptional revenue/capital receipts and payments, and drawings).[K]			
				(i)	bank deposits
				(ii)	money- market deposits
	(c)	Describe the relationship between cash flow accounting and accounting for income and expenditure. [K]		(iii)	certificates of deposit
				(iv)	government stock
				(v)	local authority stock
	(d)	Distinguish between the cash flow pattern of different types of organisations.[S]		(c)	Explain different ways of raising finance from a bank and the basic terms and conditions associated with each financing.[K]

F	**SPREADSHEETS**	
1	**Spreadsheet system overview**	**Chapter 19**
	(a) Explain the role and features of a computer spreadsheet system.[K]	
	(b) Identify applications for computer spreadsheets in cost and management accounting.[S]	
2	**Using computer spreadsheets**	**Chapter 19**
	(a) Identify what numerical and other information is needed in spreadsheets, show how information should be structured and explain security issues.[S]	
	(b) Identify and use a wide range of formulae to meet specified requirements (basic calculation formulae, relative/absolute cell reference, Round, PV, NPV, IRR and simple logical (IF) functions).[S]	
	(c) Identify and correct errors in formulas.[S]	
	(d) Identify data from different sources and demonstrate how they should be linked and combined.[S]	
3	**Presenting information in spreadsheets**	
		Chapter 19
	(a) Explain and illustrate methods of summarizing and analysing spreadsheet data (including sorting, ranking, filter, splitting screen and freezing titles).[K]	
	(b) Analyse charts and graphs (bar, line, pie, column, area and scatter).[S]	
	(c) Differentiate ways of presenting information to meet particular needs (including formatting and printing).[S]	

NOTE:

Outcomes marked with a [K] are areas where knowledge is needed. This means that you might be asked to explain the area, but you would never have to apply it in a question.

Outcomes marked with an [S] are areas where some practical skills will be needed. So you may need to apply the skill to a brief exam scenario.

THE EXAMINATION

Format of the examination

Number of marks

50 objective test questions (multiple choice, number entry and multiple response)   100

Each question is worth two marks each.

Questions assess all parts of the syllabus and will include both computational and non computational elements.

Total time allowed: 2 hours

Examination technique

- You can take a CBE **at any time during the year** – you do not need to wait for June and December exam sessions.

- Be sure you **understand how to use the software** before you start the exam. If in doubt, ask the assessment centre staff to explain it to you. **Questions are displayed on the screen** and **answers are entered using keyboard and mouse**.

- Don't panic if you realise you've answered a question incorrectly – **you can always go back and change your answer.**

- Read the questions carefully and work through any calculations required. If you don't know the answer, eliminate those options you know are incorrect and see if the answer becomes more obvious. Remember that only one answer to a multiple-choice question can be right!

- If you are sitting a paper-based examination, remember that before you finish, you must **fill in the required information** on the front of your answer booklet.

- If you are sitting a computer based examination, at the end of the examination, **you are given a certificate showing the result** you have achieved.

STUDY SKILLS AND REVISION GUIDANCE

Preparing to study

Set your objectives

Before starting to study decide what you want to achieve – the type of pass you wish to obtain.

This will decide the level of commitment and time you need to dedicate to your studies.

Devise a study plan

Determine when you will study.

Split these times into study sessions.

Put the sessions onto a study plan making sure you cover the course, course assignments and revision.

Stick to your plan!

Effective study techniques

Use the **SQR3** method

Survey the chapter – look at the headings and read the introduction, summary and objectives. Get an overview of what the text deals with.

Question – during the survey, ask yourself the questions that you hope the chapter will answer for you.

Read through the chapter thoroughly, answering the questions and meeting the objectives. Attempt the exercises and activities, and work through all the examples.

Recall – at the end of the chapter, try to recall the main ideas of the chapter without referring to the text. Do this a few minutes after the reading stage.

Review – check that your recall notes are correct.

Use the **MURDER** method

Mood – set the right mood.

Understand – issues covered and make note of any uncertain bits.

Recall – stop and put what you have learned into your own words.

Digest – go back and reconsider the information.

Expand – read relevant articles and newspapers.

Review – go over the material you covered to consolidate the knowledge.

KAPLAN PUBLISHING

While studying...

Summarise the key points of the chapter.

Make linear notes – a list of headings, divided up with subheadings listing the key points. Use different colours to highlight key points and keep topic areas together.

Try mind-maps – put the main heading in the centre of the paper and encircle it. Then draw short lines radiating from this to the main sub-headings, which again have circles around them. Continue the process from the sub-headings to sub-sub-headings, etc.

Revision

The best approach to revision is to **revise the course as you work through it**.

Also try to leave **four to six weeks before the exam for final revision**.

Make sure you **cover the whole syllabus**.

Pay special attention to **those areas where your knowledge is weak**.

If you are stuck on a topic find somebody (a tutor) to explain it to you.

Read around the subject – read good newspapers and professional journals, especially ACCA's *Student Accountant* – this can give you an advantage in the exam.

Read through the text and your notes again. Maybe put key revision points onto index cards to look at when you have a few minutes to spare.

Practise exam standard questions under timed conditions. Attempt all the different styles of questions you may be asked to answer in your exam.

Review any assignments you have completed and look at where you lost marks – put more work into those areas where you were weak.

Ensure you **know the structure of the exam** – how many questions and of what type they are.

MATHEMATICAL TABLES

Present value table

Converts future cash flows into present values

Present value of 1 i.e. $(1+r)^{-n}$

where r = discount rate

  n = number of periods until payment

Periods (n)	1%	2%	3%	4%	5%	6%	7%	8%	9%	10%	
1	0.990	0.980	0.971	0.962	0.952	0.943	0.935	0.926	0.917	0.909	1
2	0.980	0.961	0.943	0.925	0.907	0.890	0.873	0.857	0.842	0.826	2
3	0.971	0.942	0.915	0.889	0.864	0.840	0.816	0.794	0.772	0.751	3
4	0.961	0.924	0.888	0.855	0.823	0.792	0.763	0.735	0.708	0.683	4
5	0.951	0.906	0.863	0.822	0.784	0.747	0.713	0.681	0.650	0.621	5
6	0.942	0.888	0.837	0.790	0.746	0.705	0.666	0.630	0.596	0.564	6
7	0.933	0.871	0.813	0.760	0.711	0.665	0.623	0.583	0.547	0.513	7
8	0.923	0.853	0.789	0.731	0.677	0.627	0.582	0.540	0.502	0.467	8
9	0.914	0.837	0.766	0.703	0.645	0.592	0.544	0.500	0.460	0.424	9
10	0.905	0.820	0.744	0.676	0.614	0.558	0.508	0.463	0.422	0.386	10
11	0.896	0.804	0.722	0.650	0.585	0.527	0.475	0.429	0.388	0.350	11
12	0.887	0.788	0.701	0.625	0.557	0.497	0.444	0.397	0.356	0.319	12
13	0.879	0.773	0.681	0.601	0.530	0.469	0.415	0.368	0.326	0.290	13
14	0.870	0.758	0.661	0.577	0.505	0.442	0.388	0.340	0.299	0.263	14
15	0.861	0.743	0.642	0.555	0.481	0.417	0.362	0.315	0.275	0.239	15

(n)	11%	12%	13%	14%	15%	16%	17%	18%	19%	20%	
1	0.901	0.893	0.885	0.877	0.870	0.862	0.855	0.847	0.840	0.833	1
2	0.812	0.797	0.783	0.769	0.756	0.743	0.731	0.718	0.706	0.694	2
3	0.731	0.712	0.693	0.675	0.658	0.641	0.624	0.609	0.593	0.579	3
4	0.659	0.636	0.613	0.592	0.572	0.552	0.534	0.516	0.499	0.482	4
5	0.593	0.567	0.543	0.519	0.497	0.476	0.456	0.437	0.419	0.402	5
6	0.535	0.507	0.480	0.456	0.432	0.410	0.390	0.370	0.352	0.335	6
7	0.482	0.452	0.425	0.400	0.376	0.354	0.333	0.314	0.296	0.279	7
8	0.434	0.404	0.376	0.351	0.327	0.305	0.285	0.266	0.249	0.233	8
9	0.391	0.361	0.333	0.308	0.284	0.263	0.243	0.225	0.209	0.194	9
10	0.352	0.322	0.295	0.270	0.247	0.227	0.208	0.191	0.176	0.162	10
11	0.317	0.287	0.261	0.237	0.215	0.195	0.178	0.162	0.148	0.135	11
12	0.286	0.257	0.231	0.208	0.187	0.168	0.152	0.137	0.124	0.112	12
13	0.258	0.229	0.204	0.182	0.163	0.145	0.130	0.116	0.104	0.093	13
14	0.232	0.205	0.181	0.160	0.141	0.125	0.111	0.099	0.088	0.078	14
15	0.209	0.183	0.160	0.140	0.123	0.108	0.095	0.084	0.074	0.065	15

Annuity table

— Addition of the various years of cash flow

Present value of an annuity of 1 i.e. $\dfrac{1-(1+r)^{-n}}{r}$

where   r   = discount rate

   n   = number of periods

Periods — **Discount rate (r)**

(n)	1%	2%	3%	4%	5%	6%	7%	8%	9%	10%	
1	0.990	0.980	0.971	0.962	0.952	0.943	0.935	0.926	0.917	0.909	1
2	1.970	1.942	1.913	1.886	1.859	1.833	1.808	1.783	1.759	1.736	2
3	2.941	2.884	20829	2.775	2.723	2.673	2.624	2.577	2.531	2.487	3
4	3.902	3.808	3.717	3.630	3.546	3.465	3.387	3.312	3.240	3.170	4
5	4.853	4.713	4.580	4.452	4.329	4.212	4.100	3.993	3.890	3.791	5
6	5.795	5.601	5.417	5.242	5.076	4.917	4.767	4.623	4.486	4.355	6
7	6.728	6.472	6.230	6.002	5.786	5.582	5.389	5.206	5.033	4.868	7
8	7.652	7.325	7.020	6.733	6.463	6.210	5.971	5.747	5.535	5.335	8
9	8.566	8.162	7.786	7.435	7.108	6.802	6.515	6.247	5.995	5.759	9
10	9.471	8.983	8.530	8.111	7.722	7.360	7.024	6.710	6.418	6.145	10
11	10.37	9.787	9.253	8.760	8.306	7.887	7.499	7.139	6.805	6.495	11
12	11.26	10.58	9.954	9.385	8.863	8.384	7.943	7.536	7.161	6.814	12
13	12.13	11.35	10.63	9.986	9.394	8.853	8.358	7.904	7.487	7.103	13
14	13.00	12.11	11.30	10.56	9.899	9.295	8.745	8.244	7.786	7.367	14
15	13.87	12.85	11.94	11.12	10.38	9.712	9.108	8.559	8.061	7.606	15

(n)	11%	12%	13%	14%	15%	16%	17%	18%	19%	20%	
1	0.901	0.893	0.885	0.877	0.870	0.862	0.855	0.847	0.840	0.833	1
2	1.713	1.690	1.668	1.647	1.626	1.605	1.585	1.566	1.547	1.528	2
3	2.444	2.402	2.361	2.322	2.283	2.246	2.210	2.174	2.140	2.106	3
4	3.102	3.037	2.974	2.914	2.855	2.798	2.743	2.690	2.639	2.589	4
5	3.696	3.605	3.517	3.433	3.352	3.274	3.199	3.127	3.058	2.991	5
6	4.231	4.111	3.998	3.889	3.784	3.685	3.589	3.498	3.410	3.326	6
7	4.712	4.564	4.423	4.288	4.160	4.039	3.922	3.812	3.706	3.605	7
8	5.146	4.968	4.799	4.639	4.487	4.344	4.207	4.078	3.954	3.837	8
9	5.537	5.328	5.132	4.946	4.772	4.607	4.451	4.303	4.163	4.031	9
10	5.889	5.650	5.426	5.216	5.019	4.833	4.659	4.494	4.339	4.192	10
11	6.207	5.938	5.687	5.453	5.234	5.029	4.836	4.656	4.486	4.327	11
12	6.492	6.194	5.918	5.660	5.421	5.197	4.988	4.793	4.611	4.439	12
13	6.750	6.424	6.122	5.842	5.583	5.342	5.118	4.910	4.715	4.533	13
14	6.982	6.628	6.302	6.002	5.724	5.468	5.229	5.008	4.802	4.611	14
15	7.191	6.811	6.462	6.142	5.847	5.575	5.324	5.092	4.876	4.675	15

Chapter 1

MANAGEMENT INFORMATION

This chapter describes the nature and purpose of management information, and the use of accounting information within a management information system. It also describes the use of responsibility accounting, with cost centres, profit centres and investment centres, and the role of IT in the provision of management information. This chapter covers syllabus areas A1.

CONTENTS

1. Purpose of management information
2. Data and information
3. Qualities of useful management information
4. Sources of data for management accounting
5. The nature of internal reporting
6. Cost centres, profit centres and investment centres
7. IT and management accounting
8. The role of the trainee accountant

LEARNING OUTCOMES

At the end of this chapter you should be able to:

- Discuss the purpose of management information: planning, control and decision making
- Describe the features of useful management information
- Discuss the nature, source and importance of both financial and non-financial information for managers
- Describe management responsibilities for cost, profit and investment and their effect on management information and performance measurement

- Explain the role of information technology in management information
- Explain the role of the trainee accountant
- Identify suitable formats for the presentation of management information according to purpose.

1 PURPOSE OF MANAGEMENT INFORMATION

1.1 THE ROLE OF MANAGERS

Managers within any organisation are decision-makers. They have to make decisions about what should be done, and then issue instructions based on the decisions they have taken.

Decisions can be categorised as planning decisions and control decisions.

- **Planning decisions** are about what should be done. These can be decisions for the long-term or for the shorter-term. Many organisations try to work within the framework of an annual plan or budget. Much planning is done on a day-to-day or week-by-week basis and some planning, known as strategic planning, can be for longer periods ahead.

- **Control decisions** relate to monitoring what is actually happening, and if anything seems to be going wrong, deciding what should be done to correct the problem.

Many organisations produce or revise their forward planning annually, in the form of a budget. The budget cycle is illustrated in the following diagram.

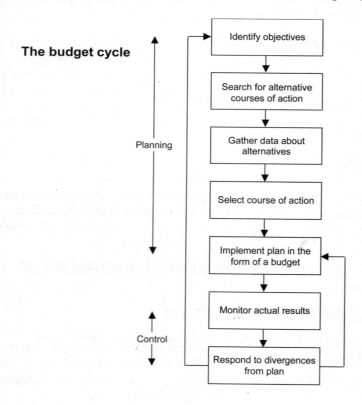

Identifying objectives

The first stage in a planning process is to identify the objectives; in other words, it is important to decide what the organisation is trying to achieve. Should it be trying to increase sales and profits, and if so by how much? Which products or services should it be trying to sell?

Assessing alternative action plans and selecting the preferred plan

There might be several ways of achieving the objectives. For example, sales and profits can be increased by raising selling prices, cutting costs or introducing new products or services to sell to customers. Alternative courses of action should be identified and evaluated. When they have been compared and evaluated the preferred course of action is selected and implemented.

Example

Suppose the objective of an organisation is to increase production by 10%. The following alternative courses of action might be identified to achieve the 10% increase.

(a) Increase the workforce by 10% and introduce a night shift. Premium wage rates would have to be paid to the night-shift workers. Machinery servicing and maintenance costs will probably increase.

(b) Replace the existing machines with modern machines with a higher capacity and train existing staff how to use the new machines.

Information would be gathered for each of these alternatives. In particular, management would want to know how much each option would cost. Much of the information will be financial (the effect on costs) but some important information will be non-financial in nature (e.g. the attitude of the workforce to shift working, or to using new machines).

Implement plan

A long-term plan usually communicates an organisation's objectives and how they are to be achieved over a 5–10 year period. This plan is then broken down into annual targets or budgets, and annual budgets might be broken down further into month-by-month plans and targets. The budget communicates detailed plans to managers within the organisation.

Monitoring actual results

When the plan is put into action, actual results should be monitored and compared with the targets. Managers need to know whether the targets will be achieved (or exceeded) and if not, by how much are actual results short of budget, and for what reasons.

The results obtained by the comparison of actual and budget performance are reported to management as part of a 'feedback' process.

Responses to divergences: taking control action

When actual results differ significantly from the budget or plan, a manager responsible for achieving the results should be required to take control measures. Control is an integral part of the planning cycle.

MA 2 : MANAGING COSTS AND FINANCES

1.2 INFORMATION AND DECISION MAKING

Management need information to help them to make decisions.

- Information for planning comes from a variety of sources, both inside and outside the organisation. Information about what the organisation has achieved in the past is often a starting point for making plans for the future. For example, knowing what a process or operation has cost in the past can be very useful for estimating the likely costs in the future.

- Information for control is largely obtained from internal sources within the organisation. Managers need to know what actual results have been achieved, in order to compare what has happened so far with what had been planned, and also in order to re-think what is likely to happen in the future unless corrective measures are taken.

A large amount of management information is financial in nature, although non-financial information can be just as important. In particular, managers need to know how much activities cost, and how much it costs to make and sell the products or services that the organisation provides to its customers.

This text will look at the nature of information about costs: how it is gathered, analysed and presented to management to help them with decision making. Cost accountants or management accountants have the job of providing information to managers about costs and profits. For the purpose of this text, cost accounting and management accounting can be taken to mean the same thing, which is the provision of management information about costs and profits.

2 DATA AND INFORMATION

A distinction can be made between data and information.

- Data is a collection of unprocessed facts or opinions.

- Information is data that has been processed so that it has a purpose and meaning.

Managers need information not data. The cost accountant processes data about expenditures into meaningful figures about the costs of products, services and processes. A simple example might help to illustrate the difference between data and information.

Example

Suppose that a departmental manager wants to know how many of the department's staff have been employed for three years or longer.

The raw data for obtaining this information would come from the employment records of each of the department's employees, which should show when the individual started in the job. This raw data would then be processed to identify how many have been employed for three years or longer, and the information presented to the departmental manager might be: '25 out of 50 of the department's employees have been in their job for over three years, representing 50% of the department's staff'.

In cost accounting, raw data consists of expenditure transactions and sales invoices, and management information consists of items such as the costs of manufacturing an item or providing a service, the profitability of a product or the cost per unit of an item, and so on.

Data has no value to management, whereas information should have a value. However, there is a cost involved in processing data into management information.

MANAGEMENT INFORMATION : CHAPTER 1

3 QUALITIES OF USEFUL MANAGEMENT INFORMATION

Information is provided to management to assist them with planning, control and decision making. Management decisions are likely to be better when they are supported by better quality information.

'Good quality' information has several characteristics.

- It should have a **purpose**, and be **relevant** for that purpose.

  There is no point in providing a manager with a report if the manager does not know why he has been given it, or what he is expected to do with it. Similarly, the information within a report should be relevant to its purpose and should not contain details that can be ignored.

- It should be **timely**. This means that it should be provided to a manager in time for the manager to do something with it. For example, suppose that a business produces monthly performance reports for its cost centres, and that in May the manager of cost centre X receives a report about actual costs incurred by the centre in January. This information would be over three months old, and the cost centre manager is likely to ignore it because it is not relevant to his current situation.

  Similarly, suppose that a senior management team want to decide on their strategy for overseas expansion, and ask for a report on market conditions in Southern Africa. If they want to make their decision in February, a report submitted in March will be of no value, because the decision will already have been taken.

- It should be **understandable**. A manager should be able to understand what the information is telling him. If he doesn't understand it, he will not use it to make a decision. If he misunderstands it, he might make a bad decision. There can be a particular problem with the use of technical language ('jargon'), and accountants should always be careful about the way in which they present financial information to non-financial managers.

- Information should be **as accurate as it needs to be**. The degree of accuracy required will depend on the reason why the information is needed. A problem in accounting can be that reports are produced showing figures to the nearest pound or dollar, when managers are only interested in figures to the nearest hundred thousand or ten thousand. On the other hand, when calculating the cost of a unit of product manufactured in a factory, managers might want the cost to be accurate to the nearest penny or cent.

- Information should be **as complete as it needs to be**, but it should **not be excessive**. Managers should be given all the information they need to make their decisions, but it is often helpful to draw their attention to what seems significant. In control reports, for example, actual results might be compared with planned results, with differences between actual and plan reported as 'variances'.

  A report that highlights the most significant information, such as the biggest variances, can help to draw management attention to what is important. Sometimes, management only want to be informed when something exceptional or out-of-the-ordinary has happened. Reporting on this basis is called **reporting by exception**.

KAPLAN PUBLISHING

- Information should be **communicated to the right person**. Within a business, management information should be directed to the manager or managers who can use it and do something with it. For example, information about costs and revenues should be reported to the manager responsible, who is in a position to control them. There is little value to be gained in reporting costs to a manager who has no control over them.

- Information should be **communicated by an appropriate channel**. A 'channel' of information refers to the method by which the information is given, such as verbally, in a formal report, in an informal report, by email, by electronic file transfer, and so on. It also refers to the individual or department or external organisation that provides the information.

  The appropriate channel of communication varies according to circumstances and the nature of the information. For example, it will depend on how quickly it is needed, how much information has to be communicated, how far the information has to be sent and the costs of sending it in different ways.

  Here are some examples.

Information	Channel of communication
A fire breaks out in the stores area.	The information must be transmitted immediately, using a fire alarm, internal and external telephone.
A cutting machine becomes badly adjusted and starts to produce components that are too short.	The machine operator must communicate verbally with his or her superior immediately. It would be wasteful to wait for the routine daily or weekly inspection.
An accounts clerk is processing petty cash vouchers from several departments that have not been properly authorised by the office manager.	The most efficient method of communicating information to several people internally, as is required in this case, is by email. However, before sending out an email, the effect on people's behaviour must be estimated. It would usually be appropriate to see people individually first in order to explain company policy.
Summary results of a subsidiary company in India need to be sent to the head office in the UK for consolidation.	A data file can be sent by email or a hard copy report could be sent by facsimile (fax).
A telephone order clerk needs to check the availability of an item of inventory before accepting a customer order.	One of the most efficient methods is to give the clerk a keyboard and screen connected to the computer system, which allows for direct interrogation of inventory levels.

3.1 THE VALUE OF INFORMATION

Another quality of good management information is that **the value of the information to management should exceed the cost of producing it**.

Management information has a value because it helps a manager to make decisions. If a decision by a manager is different from what it would have been without the information, the value of the information could be measured by the amount of money that has been saved as a result. The **value of information** results from actions by decision makers who use the information to improve profitability.

Here are some examples.

Reducing unnecessary costs	An investigation into the causes of unexpectedly high costs may uncover inefficiencies and wastage that can be eliminated in future. If a manager is not even informed that costs are running in excess of what they should be, he will not take any corrective action, and the excess spending will carry on.
Adopting better marketing strategies	Modern point-of-sales terminals in stores and supermarkets provide detailed analysis of sales by product. This information can be used to direct management attention to the products and store locations with the highest profit potential.
Better analysis of 'cost drivers'	With detailed information about the causes of costs and the factors which 'drive costs', more realistic budgets can be set. This in turn should result in scarce resources being applied in the most profitable way.

Information has a value as a strategic resource, and an efficient management information system can give a company a strategic advantage over its competitors. Information has no value if it is not used. Neither has it any value if it is known already (no 'surprise value'). In order to assess the value of information, the following questions can be asked:

- Who uses the information?
- What is it used for?
- How often is it used?
- How often is it provided but not used?
- What is achieved by its use?
- Are there alternatives to this source of information?

3.2 THE COST OF INFORMATION

The cost of producing information includes:

- the cost of gathering data
- the cost of processing data
- the cost of storing data and information
- the costs of providing the information
- the opportunity cost of management time.

In a business, management information systems can be very expensive, with large computer systems and databases, and large numbers of employees whose job it is to process and provide the information. These include management accountants. There might also be external costs, such as the cost of using a market research agency or a firm of management consultants.

4 SOURCES OF DATA FOR MANAGEMENT ACCOUNTING

Data for preparing management information comes from a variety of sources, both within the organisation (internal sources) and from outside the organisation (external sources).

4.1 INTERNAL SOURCES

There are many internal data sources for management accounting, not all of which are part of the accounting system. The boundaries of an accounting system are not always clearly defined, particularly in management accounting. The following internal accounting sources may be used.

Source	Information obtainable from the data
Sales ledger system	Number and value of invoices Volume of sales Value of sales, analysed by customer or product Receivables by age
Purchase ledger system	Number and value of invoices Value of purchases, analysed by supplier Payables by age
Payroll system	Number of employees Hours worked Time lost through sickness Wages earned Tax deducted
Records of non-current assets	Date of purchase Initial cost Location Depreciation method and rate Service history Production capacity

In addition the following internal, non-accounting sources may be used.

Source	Information available from the data
Production records	Machine breakdown times Output achieved Number of rejected units
Sales and marketing records	Types of customer Market research results Demand patterns, seasonal variations, etc.

4.2 EXTERNAL SOURCES

In addition to the internal information sources, information can be obtained from a wide range of external sources, as illustrated below.

Source	Information
Suppliers	Product prices Product specifications
Newspapers, journals	Share price Information on competitors Technological developments

Source	Information
Government	Industry statistics
	Taxation policy
	Inflation rates
Customers	Product requirements
	Price sensitivity
Employees	Wage demands
	Working conditions

ACTIVITY 1

Suppose that you are a manager in a general hospital. List some of the cost information that you might want to know about and have reported to you.

For a suggested answer, see the 'Answers' section at the end of the book.

4.3 FINANCIAL AND NON-FINANCIAL INFORMATION

It should be noted that much of the data collected will be of a non-financial nature. For example, if you examine the information coming from the payroll system above we can divide this as follows:

Financial Information	Non-Financial Information
Wages earned	Number of employees
Tax deducted	Hours worked
	Time lost through sickness

Both elements are of equal importance to managers for their planning, control and decision making purposes.

5 THE NATURE OF INTERNAL REPORTING

Management accounting (and cost accounting) differs from financial accounting because:

- the financial accounts provide the data for preparing financial statements for external users, such as a company's shareholders or the government (tax authorities)

- management accounting/cost accounting reports are prepared exclusively for internal use by management.

Internally-produced information can be provided to managers:

- in as much or as little detail as management require

- relating to whatever items management need information about

- in whatever format is preferred (for example, there are no regulations about how management accounting statements should be formatted and presented)

- as frequently or infrequently as management require.

5.1 REPORTS AND THE PRESENTATION OF INFORMATION

Information is generally supplied to management in the form of reports. Reports may be produced in a number of forms ranging from periodic printed reports, through to a senior executive producing an individual report on an executive information system.

Typical reports produced in a medium-sized manufacturing company might include the following:

Type of activity	Typical reports
Production and material control	Forward loading plans for production cycles Machine capacity forecast Departmental operating statements Inventory and work-in-progress reports Wastage report Labour utilisation report
Marketing, including distribution	Market surveys Order reports by product and geographical area Discount trends Transport and warehouse cost statements Salesperson performance Product service and support costs
Personnel	Numbers employed by category Overtime hours Sickness, absence, lateness Training requirements Career development plans Recruitment policy Job descriptions
Financial and management accounting	Annual statutory accounts Budgets and forecasts Sales and contribution analyses Cash management and working capital evaluation Capital project appraisal Standard cost and variance analysis reports Returns to government departments, e.g. returns for Sales Tax (VAT returns in the UK)

5.2 WRITING REPORTS

You might be required to prepare a short report for presentation to a manager. There are a number of general principles to apply when writing a report.

Conciseness

The report itself should be concise, avoiding unnecessary length and unnecessary detail. Managers like to see the essential features of a report quickly, and to do this, they need short reports that they can read quickly.

Any detailed statements and tables should form appendices to the main report rather than being included in the main body of the report. If such statements are numerous they should be clearly numbered in appendices for ease of reference. The main conclusions and recommendations, if any, should be summarised and highlighted separately in the report.

Structure

The report should be broken down into logical sections with a heading for each section. These should be numbered for easy reference, particularly if the report is quite lengthy.

Style

Short sentences expressed in simple and clear language are preferable to long and elaborate sentences. The aim is to communicate quickly and unambiguously, not to entertain. Opinion must be clearly separated from facts.

Presentation

The report should have a descriptive title. It should also indicate who the report is being addressed to, who has written it and the date of the report. Any terms of reference should be included at the beginning of the report.

Using graphics to improve presentation

Modern software packages make it easy to create graphs, charts, diagrams and other graphic elements from numerical data. These can enhance the appearance of a report as well as improving clarity and impact. For example, a report discussing sales trends over the last few accounting periods could be illustrated by any or all of the following visual aids:

- a bar chart analysing sales by product category

- a line graph showing the ups and downs of sales levels over the period

- a pie chart analysing sales by geographical destination.

6 COST CENTRES, PROFIT CENTRES AND INVESTMENT CENTRES

The nature of internal reporting systems will vary according to the way the organisation is structured, and the responsibilities that different managers are given. Within businesses, the focus of attention is largely on profit, and managers are held accountable for the revenues earned by their team or department, or the costs they incur.

6.1 RESPONSIBILITY ACCOUNTING

Definition **Responsibility accounting** is a system of providing financial information to management, where the structure of the reporting system is based on identifying individual parts of a business which are the responsibility of a single manager.

Definition **Responsibility centre.** A responsibility centre is an individual part of a business whose manager has personal responsibility for its performance.

Many businesses are structured into a hierarchy of responsibility centres. These might be called cost centres and revenue centres, profit centres and investment centres.

- At the 'lowest level' of structured financial reporting, there are cost centres and revenue centres. Their managers are responsible for the costs incurred by their centre or the revenues earned by the centre.

- At a higher level, there might be profit centres. Their managers are responsible for both the revenues and the costs of the centre, and so are accountable for the profit or loss the centre makes.

- At the highest level in the reporting hierarchy, there might be investment centres. In a large group of companies, an investment centre might be an entire subsidiary company, or even several subsidiary companies (a 'strategic business unit'). The manager is responsible not only for the revenues, costs and profits of the centre, but also for its capital investments and the return on investment it achieves.

6.2 COST CENTRE

Definition A **cost centre** can be defined as 'a production or service location, function, activity or item of equipment whose costs may be accumulated and attributed to cost units'.

For example, cost centres in a manufacturing company might be the machining department, the assembly department and the finishing department. Other cost centres might be order handling and despatch, stores and warehousing, and transport. Within the accounting system, the costs incurred by a cost centre are charged to that centre, so that information can be gathered about the total costs it has incurred.

The performance of a cost centre manager is judged on the extent to which cost targets have been achieved.

MANAGEMENT INFORMATION : CHAPTER 1

6.3 REVENUE CENTRE

Definition A **revenue centre** is a part of the organisation that earns sales revenue. Its manager is responsible for the revenue earned, but not for the costs of the operation.

Revenue centres are therefore generally associated with selling activities, and within a company, the sales teams under each regional sales manager might be treated as responsibility centres. Each regional manager would have sales targets to reach, and would be held responsible for the achievement of those targets.

The management information system must therefore be capable of tracing all sales revenue earned to the individual revenue centres.

6.4 PROFIT CENTRE

Definition A **profit centre** is a part of the business for which both the costs incurred and the revenues earned are identified.

The performance of a profit centre manager is measured in terms of the profit made by the centre. The profit centre performance can also be measured in terms of profit per unit, profit margins and by comparing actual profit with target profit. The manager must therefore be responsible for both costs and revenues, and in a position to plan and control both. He or she is therefore likely to have a substantial amount of authority.

Profit centres are often found in large organisations with a divisionalised structure, and each division is treated as a profit centre. Within each profit centre, there could be several cost centres and revenue centres.

When a business has a profit centre structure, data for revenues and costs must be collected and attributed to the appropriate profit centres. This data is then used to measure profit trends, profit per unit, profit margins and to compare actual profit with target profit.

6.5 INVESTMENT CENTRE

Definition The CIMA *Official Terminology* defines an **investment centre** as 'a profit centre with additional responsibilities for capital investment and possibly for financing, and whose performance is measured by its return on investment'.

An investment centre might include several profit centres.

Managers of investment centres are responsible not just for decisions affecting revenues and costs, but also for investment decisions. They should therefore be accountable not just for profits, but also for the performance of the capital invested. Performance is measured in terms of the profit relative to the level of investment. In its simplest form, this means monitoring return on capital employed (ROCE).

$$\text{ROCE} = \frac{\text{Profit}}{\text{Capital employed}}$$

To operate an investment centre system, it is necessary to collect data to provide information on costs, revenues and amounts invested (assets less liabilities).

KAPLAN PUBLISHING

Example

An investment centre has recorded the following information:

	20X5 ($000)	20X6 ($000)
Profit	180	234
Capital employed	1,000	1,200
Sales	2,000	2,400

The performance of the investment centre can be measured by calculating the ROCE and the secondary ratios, net profit margin and asset turnover.

	20X5		20X6	
ROCE	$\frac{180}{1,000}$ = 18%		$\frac{234}{1,200}$ = 19.5%	
Net profit margin	$\frac{180}{2,000}$ = 9%		$\frac{234}{2,400}$ = 9.75%	
Asset turnover	$\frac{2,000}{1,000}$ = 2		$\frac{2,400}{1,200}$ = 2	

The return earned by the investment centre has increased from 18% to 19.5%. This has been achieved by increasing the net profit margin from 9% to 9.75%, either by increasing sales or by reducing costs. The asset turnover has remained the same at 2, which means that the same sales are being generated for each $ of capital employed.

Overall performance could be compared with other similar investment centres.

6.6 THE LINK BETWEEN ROCE, NET PROFIT MARGIN AND ASSET TURNOVER

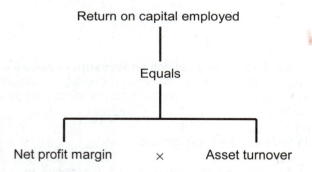

ROCE = net profit margin × asset turnover

For example, we can calculate the ROCEs using the information in the previous paragraph as follows:

20X5 ROCE = 9% × 2 = 18% (as calculated above).

20X6 ROCE = 9.75% × 2 = 19.5% (as calculated above).

6.7 THE IMPACT OF RESPONSIBILITY ACCOUNTING ON MANAGEMENT INFORMATION AND APPRAISAL

The way in which an organisation is structured, into a hierarchy of cost centres and revenue centres, profit centres and investment centres, affects the nature of management reporting. Data has to be gathered and information provided to management that will enable managers to plan and control their area of the business, and the activities for which they are responsible.

In addition, managers will recognise that their performance as a manager will be assessed in terms of costs, revenues, profits or returns on investment for their centre. Individual managers will therefore be likely to take whatever decisions seem appropriate to optimise the results of their centre.

7 IT AND MANAGEMENT ACCOUNTING

Computer technology has transformed management information systems. Many years ago, when computers were comparatively slow and with limited storage capacity, there were severe limitations to the quantity of data that could be collected, stored and analysed. Computers were able to produce regular reports, such as monthly budget performance reports, but it was difficult for managers to interrogate a system on-line and extract up-to-date information.

Today, businesses can develop information systems with enormous processing and storage capacity, providing access to vast stores of internal and external data (e.g. through the Internet). The challenge, however, is to produce information systems that:

- are designed to provide the information that managers need, both in routine reports and through ad hoc enquiries

- provide information that has value in excess of the cost of providing it.

Small businesses might limit themselves to simple systems, to avoid the cost.

7.1 FEATURES OF IT SYSTEMS

Several features of IT systems are worth noting, in the context of management information systems.

- **Data collection**. In many businesses, data can be collected electronically, which means that large volumes of data can be gathered for analysis. For example, in stores and supermarkets, point of sale (POS) systems gather data about the goods that customers purchase, mainly through bar code readers. This data is stored and analysed to provide management with information about sales volumes for each product, for each group of products, for each storage shelf in the store or for each day and for each part of each day. This can be used to analyse customer buying patterns and preferences, and to calculate the profitability of each product sold.

- **Data files**. Computer systems can have a vast storage capacity, which means that large quantities of data can be held at a relatively small cost. With database systems, data can be structured and organised so as to make it readily accessible. Data mining techniques might also be used to extract more information from databases.

- **Speed of communication and networks.** Data can be transmitted quickly to remote locations. The Internet and more particularly business intranet systems, allow managers to access business data from a laptop computer anywhere in the world. Managers can have constant access to information.

- **Processing capability.** Data can be processed quickly. Managers with on-line access to the information systems of their business might therefore be able to ask for and obtain instant 'ad hoc' information for planning, control or ad hoc decision making purposes.

- **Computer software.** Managers have access to a wide range of software for processing data and preparing management information. In particular, spreadsheet software is used extensively for planning and forecasting. Software packages are also available for financial accounting, stores control, statistical forecasting and so on.

8 THE ROLE OF THE TRAINEE ACCOUNTANT

As part of the cost accounting team, the trainee accountant is likely to be involved in gathering and processing data to measure the costs of an organisation's activities, products or services. For example, in a manufacturing business, the trainee accountant could be involved in measuring and analysing:

- the cost of raw materials used in product manufacture
- the value of raw materials inventory
- the valuation of work-in-progress and finished goods – in other words, what are the costs of production;
- the costs of the labour used/employed in each period
- the costs of other expenses in the period
- overhead costs for each cost centre
- overhead absorption rates
- the total cost of each type of product made by the business
- the cost per unit sold
- the profitability of each product.

CONCLUSION

Measuring costs and revenues is an important first step in providing management with information to assist them with planning and control decisions. A variety of costing methods and techniques are described in the following chapters.

KEY TERMS

Responsibility accounting – a system of providing financial information to management, where the structure of the reporting system is based on identifying individual parts of a business which are the responsibility of a single manager.

Responsibility centre – an individual part of a business whose manager has personal responsibility for its performance.

Cost centre – a location, function, activity or item of equipment for which costs are accumulated and attributed to cost units.

Profit centre – a part of the business for which both the costs incurred and revenues earned are identified.

Investment centre – a profit centre which is also responsible for capital investment.

SELF TEST QUESTIONS

		Paragraph
1	What is the purpose of management information?	1.2
2	What is the difference between data and information?	2
3	List six qualities of good information.	3, 3.1
4	Define responsibility accounting.	6.1
5	Define a cost centre.	6.2
6	Define a profit centre.	6.4
7	Define an investment centre.	6.5

EXAM-STYLE QUESTIONS

1   A profit centre is:

        A   the profit attributable to a business unit

        B   a business unit whose manager is responsible for operating costs and revenues from the activities of the unit

        C   a unit of product or a service for which costs and revenues are measured

        D   a business unit whose manager is responsible for investment decisions within the unit.

2   Which of the following is always a desirable quality of information?

    A   Instant availability

    B   Complete accuracy

    C   Brevity

    D   Understandability

3   Which of the following is an example of data?

    A   A graph showing sales by product for the previous year

    B   A list of employees of an organisation

    C   A report showing the percentage of rejects by machine

    D   A table showing inflation projections by business sector

4   Information should be produced if:

    (i)   Its cost exceeds its value

    (ii)   It is relevant and timely

    (iii) It has always been produced

Which of the above statements are true?

    A   (ii) only

    B   (ii) and (iii)

    C   (i) and (iii)

    D   All of them

For the answers to these questions, see the 'Answers' section at the end of the book.

Chapter 2

COST ACCOUNTING SYSTEMS

This chapter explains the framework for a cost accounting system, and how data is captured and processed to produce information about costs for management. The features of a cost accounting system outlined in this chapter will be explained in more detail in subsequent chapters. This chapter covers syllabus area A2.

CONTENTS

1. A cost accounting system
2. Documentation for the source data
3. Cost units
4. Recording and coding of costs
5. Computer systems and cost accounting

LEARNING OUTCOMES

At the end of this chapter you should be able to:

- explain the relationship between the cost/management accounting system and the financial accounting/management information systems (including interlocking and integrated bookkeeping systems)

- describe the process of accounting for input costs and relating them to work done

- identify the documentation required, and the flow of documentation, for different cost accounting transactions

- explain the use of codes in categorising and processing transactions, and the importance of correct coding (including sequential, hierarchical, block, faceted and mnemonic coding methods)

- explain and illustrate the concept of cost units

- describe the different methods of costing final outputs and their appropriateness to different types of business organisation

- describe methods of capturing, processing, storing and outputting cost and management accounting data by computer.

1 A COST ACCOUNTING SYSTEM

Definition A **cost accounting system** is a system used by an organisation to gather, store and analyse cost data. The purpose of a cost accounting system is to provide management information about costs and profits.

A cost accounting system is often the basis for a management accounting system. The terms 'cost accounting' and 'management accounting' are often used to mean the same thing, although strictly there are some differences.

- A cost accounting system is concerned with gathering internal data about costs and revenues, whereas a management accounting system is also concerned with gathering and analysing data from external sources.

- A cost accounting system is concerned mainly with measuring actual costs and revenues, whereas a management accounting system is also concerned with providing management with forward-looking estimates and predictions.

- A cost accounting system is often based on a system of double-entry ledger accounting, whereas a management accounting system can exist without a cost ledger.

1.1 COST ACCOUNTING AND FINANCIAL ACCOUNTING SYSTEMS

Financial accounting systems have a nominal ledger, sales ledger and purchase ledger, and books of prime entry for recording transaction data before entering the data in the ledger accounts.

The cost ledger is either integrated with the nominal ledger system or supplementary to the nominal ledger system.

Definition **Integrated accounts** are a set of accounting records which provides both financial and cost accounts using a common input of data for all accounting purposes. (*CIMA, Official Terminology*)

Definition **Interlocking accounts** are a system in which the cost accounts are distinct from the financial accounts, the two sets of accounts being kept continuously in agreement by the use of control accounts or reconciled by other means. (*CIMA, Official Terminology*)

- The nominal ledger in a financial accounting system contains accounts for assets, liabilities, owners' capital, income and expenses.

- The cost ledger in a cost accounting system contains accounts for recording input elements of cost and building up the cost of items produced and sold by the organisation.

The accounts in the cost ledger take the information from the nominal ledger, and analyse it into greater detail in order to establish the costs of products, services or processes.

1.2 DIRECT COSTS AND INDIRECT COSTS

Cost accounting systems make a distinction between direct costs and indirect costs. A direct cost is an item of cost that is directly attributable to a particular cost unit, such as a particular product, service or job. An indirect cost is an item of expense that cannot be attributed directly to a specific cost unit. Indirect costs are known as **overheads**.

Overhead costs within a manufacturing organisation are commonly categorised into:

- **production overheads**, which are indirect costs relating to production activities
- **administration overheads**, which are indirect costs relating to general administration activities
- **selling and distribution overheads**, which are indirect costs relating to selling, marketing and distribution activities.

Overhead costs in a service organisation may also be categorised into functional elements in a similar way.

We will be looking at direct costs and indirect costs in more detail in the next chapter.

1.3 THE PROCESS OF ACCOUNTING FOR INPUT COSTS

Materials costs, labour costs and other expenses

There are three basic components of cost:

- materials costs
- labour costs
- other expenses.

In a cost accounting system, **transactions involving materials costs** are recorded in a **stores account**. These transactions are mainly the purchase of stores items and the issue of materials to various departments within the organisation. The stores account also records the value of opening inventory and closing inventory of materials at the beginning and end of each period. Inventory may be raw materials in a manufacturing environment or material inputs in a service environment.

Transactions involving labour costs are recorded in a **wages and salaries control account**. This account records the total cost of wages and salaries, and is used to charge these costs to different departments, as either direct labour costs or indirect labour costs (overheads).

If we assume for simplicity that all other expenses are treated as indirect costs or overheads, **transactions involving other expenses** are recorded in an overhead costs account.

Building up costs of final outputs

There are also accounts within a cost ledger for building up the costs of production and the cost of sales of the products manufactured or jobs carried out for customers. The accounts that are used to do this are:

- the **work-in-progress account**, which records the costs of items manufactured. The account records costs in total, but the costs might be broken down into the costs of individual jobs or processes or the costs of individual products. The opening balance and closing balance on this account at the start and end of a period represent the total cost of unfinished production

MA 2 : MANAGING COSTS AND FINANCES

- the **finished goods account**, which records the cost of finished production that has not yet been sold to a customer

- the **cost of sales account**, which records the cost of finished production that has been sold to customers.

Similar accounts may be used to collect the cost of providing a service but there will be no finished goods account as it is not possible to hold inventory of finished services.

1.4 THE MAIN ACCOUNTS IN THE COST LEDGER

To understand a cost accounting system, you need to be familiar with the principles of double entry bookkeeping. The following example illustrates how the double entry in a cost ledger would be carried out. Work through this to gain an overview of the approach and revisit this example after studying Chapters 3 to 8 which give you more detail on each individual account.

Example – note that this example is longer than any question that could be asked for in an exam. But it should explain all the possible entries that you could be asked to make.

A company has the following information

Opening balances of:

	Raw materials	$2,000
	Work-in-progress	$1,500
	Finished goods	$8,000

Transactions recorded in the period

Material purchases	$40,000
Direct materials issued to production	$21,000
Indirect materials issued to production	$3,000
Indirect materials issued to administration	$6,000
Indirect materials issued to selling	$5,000
Gross wages	$30,000
Of which direct wages are	$11,000
Indirect wages in production are	$7,000
Indirect wages in administration are	$4,000
Indirect wages in selling are	$8,000
Indirect production expenses	$7,500
Indirect administration expenses	$10,000
Indirect selling expenses	$3,000
Overheads charged to production	$17,500
Production completed	$49,000
Production cost of goods sold	$52,000

This information can be used to prepare the cost accounts.

The main accounts in the cost ledger are illustrated below. There are different types of account.

- Asset accounts such as the stores account, work-in-progress (WIP) account and finished goods account. These record the transactions relating to raw materials, partly finished goods and completed goods in a period. Often there is inventory of raw materials, partly finished goods and finished goods at the end of a period which result in a closing balance and a corresponding opening balance for the beginning of the next period. In our example you can see the opening balances recorded on the debit side of the accounts. Once all of the other transactions for the period have been recorded in these accounts, the closing balance can be calculated as a balancing figure on the credit side.

COST ACCOUNTING SYSTEMS : CHAPTER 2

- Expense accounts such as wages and overheads accounts. The stores account also records any purchases of raw materials in the period. Total costs for the period are debited to these accounts. The costs are then analysed according to whether they are direct or indirect costs. Direct costs are transferred to the WIP account and indirect costs are passed to the relevant overhead accounts. Normally you would not expect to see a closing balance on a wages account as all of the labour costs incurred are allocated in the period. In our example you can see the costs incurred in the period debited to the stores, wages and overhead accounts. The analysis into direct and indirect costs and the resulting accounting treatment will be covered in more detail in later chapters.

In the example you can see that the WIP account collects all of the costs relating to the production of the cost units in the period. As the goods are completed the value of the finished goods is credited to the WIP account and debited to the finished goods account.

The cost of goods sold is then credited to the finished goods account and debited to the cost of sales account.

Stores account

	$		$
Opening inventory	2,000	Work-in-progress	21,000
Creditors account	40,000	(Direct materials issued to production)	
(Material purchases)		Production overheads	3,000
		Admin overheads	6,000
		Selling/dist'n overheads	5,000
		(Indirect materials consumed)	
		Closing inventory (Balancing figure)	7,000
	42,000		42,000

Wages and salaries control account

	$		$
Bank, PAYE etc	30,000	Work-in-progress	11,000
(Total wages and salaries costs)		(Direct wages costs)	
		Production overheads	7,000
		Admin overheads	4,000
		Selling/dist'n overheads	8,000
		(Indirect labour costs)	
	30,000		30,000

KAPLAN PUBLISHING

Production overheads account

OVERHEADS INCURRED	$	OVERHEADS ABSORBED TO PRODUCTION*	$
Stores account *(Indirect production materials costs)*	3,000	Work-in-progress	17,500
Wages and salaries control *(Indirect production labour costs)*	7,000		
Bank/creditors *(Other indirect expenses)*	7,500		
	17,500		17,500

***Note:** As we shall see in a later chapter, the total amount of overheads absorbed or charged to production is often different from the total amount of overhead costs actually incurred, and there are under-absorbed or over-absorbed overhead costs.

Administration overheads account

	$		$
Stores account *(Indirect materials costs)*	6,000	Income statement	20,000
Wages and salaries control *(Admin labour costs)*	4,000		
Bank/creditors *(Other indirect expenses)*	10,000		
	20,000		20,000

Selling and distribution overheads account

	$		$
Stores account *(Indirect materials costs)*	5,000	Income statement	16,000
Wages and salaries control *(Sales and distribution labour costs)*	8,000		
Bank/creditors *(Other indirect expenses)*	3,000		
	16,000		16,000

Work-in-progress (WIP) account

	$		$
Opening inventory *(Unfinished production)*	1,500	Finished goods	49,000
Stores account *(Direct materials costs)*	21,000		
Wages and salaries control *(Direct labour costs)*	11,000		
Production overhead account *(Indirect production costs)*	17,500	Closing inventory *(Unfinished production – Balancing figure)*	2,000
	51,000		51,000

Finished goods account

	$		$
Opening inventory *(Unsold finished production)*	8,000	Cost of sales *(Production cost of finished goods sold in the period)*	52,000
Work-in-progress *(Production completed in the period)*	49,000	Closing inventory *(Unsold finished production – balancing figure)*	5,000
	57,000		57,000

Cost of sales account

	$		$
Finished goods *(Production cost of finished goods sold in the period)*	52,000	Income statement	52,000
	52,000		52,000

2 DOCUMENTATION FOR THE SOURCE DATA

The details of costs incurred are obtained from source data and recorded in the costing system. The nature of the source documentation used varies between organisations. Source documents include:

	Documents	
For materials purchased	Goods received note	Confirming receipt into stores
	Purchase invoice	Details of purchase costs
For materials used	Materials requisition note	For materials issued to a particular department
	Job cost card	To record materials used in a particular job
Labour costs	Payroll records	Total labour costs, analysed between departments
	Job cost cards	Details of labour time/costs on particular jobs
	Job sheets/ job time cards	Details of time spent on different activities and costs of the time spent
Expenses	Purchase invoices	
Costs of production	Job cost cards Production analysis sheets	

Source documents will be described in more detail in later chapters.

3 COST UNITS

3.1 COST UNITS

Definition A **cost unit** is a unit of production or a unit of activity in relation to which a cost is measured. In other words, a cost unit is an item for which an output cost or an activity cost is measured.

Cost units are measured for several reasons:

- to establish how much it has cost to produce an item or perform an activity
- to measure the profit or loss on the item
- to value closing inventories of the item
- to compare actual costs of the item with budgeted costs
- to plan future costs, by basing future costs on historical costs
- to decide on a selling price for the item, where the selling price is derived by a 'cost plus' formula
- to monitor changes in costs over time.

In a manufacturing business, the cost units that are used will depend on the nature of the manufacturing process.

- When the firm manufactures different products, the cost unit will be a unit of the product, and each product will have a different cost unit.
- When a firm manufactures standard units in batches, the cost unit will be the batch of output.
- When a firm carries out jobs or contracts for customers, the cost unit will be the cost of each specific job or contract.

With service industries, or for measuring the cost of activities, cost units will vary according to the nature of the work. Here are some examples:

Activity	Cost unit
Road haulage	Tonne-mile delivered
Passenger transport	Passenger-mile
Canteen services	Meal
Hospital services (in-patient services)	Patient-day
Hotel accommodation	Guest-night
Electricity generation	Kilowatt hour generated

An average cost per unit can be calculated by dividing the total costs by the total number of units. Cost units for service industries are often composite measures, and can be difficult to identify.

4 RECORDING AND CODING OF COSTS

4.1 RECORDING COSTS

When costs are recorded, analysed and reported to management, it is important that costs should be reported to the managers or departments responsible for the spending. In other words, the reporting of cost information should ideally be based on a system of responsibility accounting and responsibility centres.

- Direct material costs can be charged directly to the production department or the job that uses the materials.

- Similarly, direct labour costs can be charged directly to the production department or the job where the work is carried out.

- Overheads, which cannot be traced directly to an output product or job, can be traced directly to a department or unit of the organisation. In other words, indirect costs can be traced to responsibility centres within the organisation.

When costs are recorded in a cost accounting system, it should therefore be possible to identify the cost with a particular production department, product, job, process or responsibility centre. Having recorded costs in this way, the process of measuring and reporting costs of output can begin.

4.2 COST CODES

When an organisation operates a cost accounting system, the system is likely to be computer-based. Transactions are recorded by input to a computerised cost accounting system (which is usually integrated with the financial accounting system). To simplify the process of entering data into the system, and subsequently analysing output costs, coding systems will be used.

Definition   A **code** is a system of symbols designed for application to a classified set of items, to give a brief accurate reference. Codes facilitate the entry of data to a system, and the collation and analysis of the data.

Cost codes are used in a costing system.

4.3 CODING SYSTEMS

There are many ways to cost codes. Here are some of the more popular methods:

Sequential Code

This is the most basic type of code. It simply means that each code follows a numerical or alphabetical sequence. Planning is needed to determine how many codes might be needed in total.

For example, let's assume we are making a coding list for different types of expenses. We could give our first category, say Motor Expenses, code 001. Our next type of expense, say Electricity, would get code 002. Each expense would then follow in sequence. This allows us to have as many as 999 different types of expenses as we are using a three digit sequential code.

Block Code

Block codes are often used to categorise sequential codes together. For example, an accounting system might have the following block codes:

0000 – Expenses

1000 – Revenue

2000 – Non-current assets

3000 – Current assets

4000 – Long term liabilities

5000 – Equity

The 3000 "Block" is allocated to Current assets. This means that it is possible to classify up to 1,000 different current assets (such as different types of inventories and bank accounts) using this block.

Hierarchical Code

This text uses an hierarchical code. Each section is given a number and each sub-section is given an added decimal number. For example, we have seen

1 A COST ACCOUNTING SYSTEM

    1.1   COST ACCOUNTING AND FINANCIAL ACCOUNTING SYSTEMS

    1.2   DIRECT COSTS AND INDIRECT COSTS

    1.3   THE PROCESS OF ACCOUNTING FOR INPUT COSTS

    1.4   THE MAIN ACCOUNTS IN THE COST LEDGER

This allows for infinite expandability. For example, if we decided to further sub-divide section 1.2 we might get the following:

    1.2   DIRECT COSTS AND INDIRECT COSTS

        1.2.1   DIRECT COSTS

        1.2.2   INDIRECT COSTS

Each sub-category simply gets a further decimal coding.

Faceted Code

A faceted code is one that is broken down into a number of facets or fields, each of which signifies a unit of information.

Consider the following simplified table which has been extracted as a sample from the faceted code used by a large international manufacturer:

Code	Region	Code	Department	Code	Expense
01	Europe	01	Sales	0244	Salaries
02	Asia	02	Production	0245	National insurance
03	USA	03	Personnel and Finance	0246	Pension contributions
04	Africa	04	Administration	0247	Bonuses

In this example, there are three facets, or fields, to the code:

Facet 1 is the region, and is 2 digits long

Facet 2 is the department, and is 2 digits long

Facet 3 is the type of expense, and is 4 digits long

If we wanted to post an expense for a bonus paid to the production department of the USA region, the code would be:

03020247

That is: 03 (for USA), 02 (for Production) and 0247 (for Bonuses).

It can be seen that a faceted system is a complicated one and requires lots of training and possibly a table such as the one above to be used for interpretation of codes. But it does allow for more sub-divisions and a greater number of codes.

Mnemonic Code

Mnemonic means something that aids the memory or understanding. This uses an alphabetical coding rather than a numerical coding system. It is often used to abbreviate or simplify information.

For example, in accounting we might use

Code	Meaning
NCA	Non Current Assets
EXP	Expenses
REV	Revenue

Mnemonic codes are a way of quickly expressing information and making that information easily understood. However, this coding method makes it very difficult to use sub-categories or to have too much information. Mnemonic coding is likely to struggle to categorise 999 different types of expenses, for example.

Conclusion   A **cost code** is designed to analyse and classify the costs of an organisation in the most appropriate manner for that organisation. There are no set methods of designing a cost code and the cost code of a particular organisation will be that which best suits the operations and costs of that business.

ACTIVITY 1

Suppose that a cost coding system is such that the first two letters of the code represent the cost centre, the third letter the type of expense and the fourth letter the detail of the expense.

Codes are as follows:

S	Salesman's expenses
ED	Eastern Division
P	Petrol

Required:

Code an Eastern Division's salesman's petrol expenses.

For a suggested answer, see the 'Answers' section at the end of the book.

4.6 PURPOSE OF COST CODES

The main purposes of cost codes are to:

(a) assist precise information: costs incurred can be associated with pre-established codes, so reducing variations in classification

(b) facilitate electronic data processing: computer analysis, summarisation and presentation of data can be performed more easily through the medium of codes

(c) facilitate a logical and systematic arrangement of costing records: accounts can be arranged in blocks of codes permitting additional codes to be inserted in logical order

(d) simplify comparison of totals of similar expenses rather than all of the individual items

(e) incorporate check codes within the main code to check the accuracy of the postings.

ACTIVITY 2

The following is a short extract from an organisation's code structure.

Cost centres

	Code
Factory	
Machine shop A	301
Machine shop B	302
Boiler house	303
Etc	
Administration	
Accounts department	401
Secretary	402
Security officers	403
Etc	
Selling	
South area	501
North area	502
East area	503
Etc	

Type of expense

Materials	
Machine lubricants	001
Cleaning supplies	002
Stationery	003
Etc	
Wages	
Supervisor's salary	051
Cleaning wages	052
Etc	
Expenses	
Depreciation of machinery	071
Insurance of machinery	072
Etc	

Required:

How would the following items be coded?

(a) A stores requisition for an issue of machine lubricant to machine shop B.

(b) The salary of an East area sales supervisor.

(c) The depreciation expense for the machine shop A machinery.

For a suggested answer, see the 'Answers' section at the end of the book.

5 COMPUTER SYSTEMS AND COST ACCOUNTING

5.1 INTRODUCTION

Cost accounting data is likely to be collected, processed and analysed using computer systems. The main elements of computer systems are:

- hardware

- software, and

- in many cases, communications links, including links to the Internet.

5.2 HARDWARE

The term 'hardware' is used to describe the equipment in a computer system, including the computer itself.

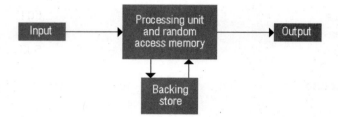

The diagram shown above can represent all computers. Data is entered through input devices, or data may be used from the backing store, and output is produced. Records on the backing store may also be updated.

Peripherals are hardware devices other than processors or networks. The term peripherals commonly refers to input, output and communication hardware. Some of these devices are covered below.

5.3 INPUT DEVICES

Examples of input hardware devices include keyboard and mouse, bar code reader, touch screen, optical mark reading, optical character recognition and a scanner.

You may be familiar with many of these devices and how they may be used to capture management accounting data.

Keyboard and mouse

A keyboard and mouse are commonly used input devices in office systems, in conjunction with visual display screens (VDUs). Many office workers, including managers, have a personal computer (PC) or other terminal on their desk top, with keyboard and mouse (or tracker ball) and the VDU for input and output.

Using a mouse is usually quicker than a keyboard, and input errors are fewer, when the computer system provides a **graphical user interface** (GUI). This is a way of presenting data and information to users, and offering processing choices to users, in the form of an easy-to-understand graphical presentation on screen. Although it is now usual for computer systems to have a GUI, the term originated because interaction between a computer user and the computer at one time was by text-and-keyboard instructions. GUI, in contrast, uses graphical displays and pull-down menus, which the computer user can control with a mouse.

For example, computer users have grown accustomed to WIMP computer system design. WIMP stands for either **Windows, Icons, Mouse and Pointer**, or **Windows, Icons, Mouse and Pull-down menus**.

Windows allows users to view two or more different programs or parts of the computer system at the same time on their screen, each in a different window or box.

Icons are used to represent data files or processing options. The computer user can choose a file or processing option by moving the screen pointer or cursor to the icon, and clicking the mouse to select the icon.

The pointer or cursor is an arrow head or similar image on the screen that can be moved around by the mouse and used for selecting options.

Pull-down menus are lists of files or processing options. Drop-down menus might be shown along the top of the VDU screen, which can be selected with the pointer and mouse. A list of choices in the menu then drops down on to the screen, from which the computer user makes a selection, also with pointer and mouse.

However, both keyboard input and input with a mouse are slow methods of input, since they are dependent on the speed of the human operator. They are inappropriate input devices for high volume, high-speed automated processing systems and, where possible, faster input methods should be preferred.

Bar code reader

A bar code is a pattern of black and white stripes representing a code, often an inventory item code.

The code is read by a scanner or light pen, which converts the bar code image into an electronic form acceptable to the computer. Bar codes are used widely at checkout points in supermarkets and shops (**point of sale systems** or **POS systems**). They allow the point of sale system to recognise the item being purchased and to add its price to the customer's total bill. They speed up the checkout process and reduce the risk of input error by the checkout clerk.

Touch screen

A touch screen is another form of point of sale device, which might be used in a cafeteria or restaurant. The screen displays a range of items that are available for sale, and the salesperson inputs the customer's order by touching the appropriate icon with a finger. The screen recognises the instruction and converts it into an electronic command for the computer.

Optical mark reading (OMR)

Optical mark reading (OMR) involves making marks, usually with a pencil or pen, on a standard document. The document is then read by an optical mark reader, and the positioning of the mark or marks on the document can be interpreted as data for processing by the computer.

MA 2 : MANAGING COSTS AND FINANCES

Optical character recognition (OCR)

With optical character recognition (OCR), a reader can recognise hand-written characters from their shape, and convert them into electronic data format. OCR applications have included meter reading forms for electricity and gas meters.

Scanner

A scanner is a device that can read any form of image and convert it into an electronic form for acceptance by a computer system. Scanners can therefore be used to input diagrams and pictures, signatures and other visual images, as well as images of text.

5.4 OUTPUT DEVICES

Output from a computer system is often stored, in which case the output is transferred to a storage device. The other most common forms of output are printer and VDU screen.

Printers

Different types of printer are available. The most commonly used are now either:

- ink-jet printers for smaller computers and low-volume output, and
- laser printers, which are capable of faster output and so can handle much higher print volumes, with high print quality.

Printers can be used for the output of diagrams and pictures as well as text, and have widespread applications in business. In some computer systems, output can be printed on the standard pre-printed stationery, to produce documents such as sales invoices and statements.

VDU screen

Output to a VDU screen is temporary, whereas printed output is more permanent. However, many computer systems rely on output to VDU, where the computer user can simply read the information provided. There are many examples of VDU output, but examples are:

- email messages, which can be printed out but are more usually read on screen
- customer service centres, where customer sales orders and queries by telephone can be handled by a customer service representative with access to central computer records through keyboard, mouse and VDU screen.

Other output devices

The other most commonly used output devices are for storing data in electronic form, and include floppy disks, compact disks or DVDs. Data can also be output onto microfilm (for which a computer output on microfilm or COM device is needed).

5.5 STORAGE DEVICES

Storage devices are devices for holding data or information (and programs) in electronic form. They are used for both input of data into a computer system and for output of data and information for storage. A distinction is made between:

Internal storage

Data and programs can be stored in the internal RAM of the computer, or in a hard disk.

RAM (random access memory) is volatile memory (i.e. the contents are lost when the computer is turned off) but it is accessible directly by the computer.

ROM (read-only memory) is non-volatile memory (i.e. the contents are not lost when the computer is turned off). ROM is a memory chip which has data permanently written onto it, hence its name (read-only memory). New data cannot be written into this memory and the original data cannot be changed.

Hard disks provide the permanent storage in a computer. The contents of memory remain intact without the need for power supply, but there is a small time delay involved in accessing data and files stored on the disks. CDs can also provide disk storage, although CD/RW drives are needed to read and write to this storage medium.

External storage

The main types of external storage are tape, floppy disks, zip disks, CDs and DVDs.

Storage capacity is measured in bytes. A byte is a unit of eight binary digits or bits, and can be used to represent one character (one number, one letter or one punctuation mark, etc).

A kilobyte (Kb) is about 1,000 bytes (it is actually 1,024 bytes).

A megabyte (Mb) is about 1,000,000 bytes (it is actually 1,024 × 1,024 bytes).

A gigabyte is about 1,000 million bytes.

The storage capacity of a standard floppy disk is 1.44 Mb. Zip disks hold data in a compressed form. With **data compression**, the data held on the file is reduced in size, so that it does not require one byte to represent one character. Zip disk drives compress the data for storage purposes and de-compress it when it is needed for processing. They have a capacity of 150 Mb, 250 Mb or 750 Mb. (Zipped files are also used for transmitting large files more quickly via the Internet.)

The storage capacity of a CD-ROM is 650 Mb, and data can be retrieved by the computer from a CD more quickly than from a floppy disk. CDs are therefore faster devices as well as having larger storage capacity. DVDs hold between 4 Gb and 15 Gb, and are faster devices than CDs.

5.6 THE CENTRAL PROCESSING UNIT (CPU)

The central processing unit (CPU) is the computer itself. It consists of several component elements:

- a control unit, which supervises and co-ordinates all the computer's processing, in accordance with its programmed instructions
- an arithmetic and logic unit, which carries out mathematical computations and logic tests on data
- internal storage or memory.

The central computer must have a small amount of ROM and some RAM. It will also have some instantly accessible permanent storage, commonly referred to as the **hard drive**.

The CPU controls all the input, output and storage devices of the computer, holds the program that is currently being worked on and executes the program instructions.

5.7 OPERATING SYSTEMS SOFTWARE

The operating system is the most important piece of software in any computer system, as without it the system will not work at all. It consists of a number of tools to allow the following functions:

- communication between the operator and the computer

- control of the processor and storage hardware

- the management of files

- the use of peripherals such as printers and modems.

When the computer is multi-tasking, and running several application programs simultaneously, the operating system allocates internal storage space to each application, chooses which programs should be run in which order of priority and decides how much CPU time to give to each application.

There are two different types of operating systems in common use in business:

- command-driven operating systems, such as DOS, which are sometimes used with a graphical user interface (GUI) utility

- WIMP (Windows®, icons, mouse and pointer) operating systems such as Windows® Vista, which have their own GUI.

The GUI allows a reduction in the amount of training required to use the system, and prevents the selection of invalid or unreasonable options or instructions.

5.8 APPLICATIONS SOFTWARE

Many computer users have the same applications. For example, any business has to have systems for word processing, payroll, sales ledger, bought ledger and inventory control. Very often the requirements for these applications are similar for a wide range of companies. An application package is a standard program, or suite of programs, designed to perform a specific task. It saves users from having to develop application programs that are essentially the same as those already developed.

Examples of applications software include spreadsheets, word processing, databases, accounting and communications packages.

Integrated packages

Some programs, or packages of programs, can perform more than one task e.g. office administration packages that comprise word processing, creating and using a database, spreadsheets and business graphics. These are called integrated packages because they bring these varied tasks together. Examples of integrated software packages include Microsoft Office® and Claris Works®.

Accounting packages

At their simplest level, accounts packages can be considered as electronic ledgers, with the routine transactions recorded on a computer system, rather than on paper, and the general principles of double entry bookkeeping being incorporated in the software.

There are many advantages in computerising an accounts system e.g. the software package **Sage Accountant Plus**® includes sales invoicing, inventory control and report generation, as well as the basic sales, purchase and nominal ledgers. The format of invoices can be set by the user as pre-printed forms and other features that can be expected from even the simplest packages would include some form of security and auditing controls. More advanced, and more expensive, packages would be expected to provide such options as payroll, multiple currency accounts, and cheque production facilities with integrated word processors and spreadsheets so that information can be used anywhere in the system and incorporated into financial modelling routines and reports or letters as required.

Desk Top Publishing (DTP)

DTP packages such as PageMaker® and InDesign® are popular as they let a user combine text and art to present reports in a much more professional-looking way. Applications for a DTP package include:

- output of financial reports, incorporating the use of high quality graphics

- the preparation of financial accounts that requires a high quality of printout

- reports used in consultancy work, which may incorporate graphs, charts, etc.

5.9 COMPUTER COMMUNICATIONS

Where an organisation has several locations, it may be more effective to process data locally rather than at one central installation. By doing this, individual managers will be able to schedule their own processing and will have more control over the contents of their database systems. Any system that requires computers to communicate with each other will need specialised hardware and software such as:

- modems

- communication programs

- local area networks (LANs).

The modem is the interface between the computer and the telephone system. In addition communications software is needed to handle the communications process.

Communication through a modem uses the public telecommunications system. This may be unnecessarily elaborate for an organisation that simply needs its own computers to be able to communicate with each other or to share a piece of expensive hardware. In these circumstances, a local area network (or LAN) may be more suitable. This consists of a circuit, which connects the computers to each other and contains the hardware needed for efficient communication (often in the form of expansion cards that plug directly into the computers' circuitry), and software to run the network.

5.10 INTERNET AND OTHER FORMS OF COMMUNICATION

Access to the Internet is invaluable for many businesses.

Information can be obtained from other organisations quickly. Examples of external information include published financial information by companies (and other investor information), government guidelines and statistics and information about the products and services of other suppliers and competitors.

An organisation can provide information about itself on its own website, including information about its products or services. Customers might be able to place orders via the Internet and even pay for the order. E-commerce, a term for buying and selling via the Internet, continues to grow rapidly.

Intranets

An intranet is a 'private' computer network operated by an organisation, usually consisting of several local area networks linked to each other by telecommunications links and in which one or more Internet servers provide a link between the network and the Internet.

Email

Electronic mail (email) allows messages and data files to be transmitted between users instantly, without the need for paper or disks as transmission media. When users are allowed to send and receive email messages to computers outside the network, the system uses the Internet.

Electronic Data Interchange (EDI)

Electronic Data Interchange or EDI is a system for enabling the computer systems of different organisations to communicate without the need for paperwork. Typically, it is used to link the purchasing and invoicing systems of suppliers and their customers. EDI is used predominantly by large business organisations.

CONCLUSION

Cost accounting systems are likely to be computerised systems, in which cost and revenue transactions are entered with identifying cost codes. Individual transactions will be traced to cost centres, and identified by type of cost. Total costs are built up within a double entry cost bookkeeping system.

Cost accounting systems vary between organisations. This chapter has introduced the main elements of these systems, which will be explained in greater detail in later chapters of this text.

KEY TERMS

Cost accounting system – a system used by an organisation to gather, store and analyse cost data.

Stores account – debited with the cost of raw material purchases and credited with materials issued.

Work-in-progress account – debited with the cost of production and credited with the cost of finished goods.

Finished goods account – debited with the cost of finished goods and credited with the cost of goods sold to customers.

Production overhead account – debited with the overhead cost incurred and credited with the overhead cost absorbed. Any balance on the account is under or over absorbed overhead.

Cost unit – a unit of production or activity for which a cost is measured.

Computer hardware – the equipment in a computer system, including input devices, output devices, the central processing unit and storage devices.

Computer software – the systems used to run the computer, including operating systems and application software.

SELF TEST QUESTIONS

		Paragraph
1	What is a cost accounting system?	1
2	Which account in a cost ledger is used to record the cost of materials purchased?	1.3
3	Which account in a cost ledger is used to record the cost of items manufactured?	1.3
4	What double entry accounting record is needed for recording the cost of completed production?	1.4
5	What double entry accounting record is needed for recording the cost of indirect materials used in production?	1.4
6	Which source document might be used to record the cost of materials taken from stores by a cost centre or for a particular job?	2
7	What is a cost unit?	3.1
8	What is the purpose of calculating the cost of cost units?	3.1
9	What is a typical cost unit for a passenger transport service?	3.1
10	What is a cost centre code?	4.3

MA 2 : MANAGING COSTS AND FINANCES

EXAM-STYLE QUESTIONS

1 If the direct labour costs in a manufacturing company are $95,000 in March, the costs would be recorded in the cost ledger as:

   A   Debit Work-in-progress $95,000, credit Wages and Salaries $95,000

   B   Debit Work-in-progress $95,000, credit Production Overheads $95,000

   C   Debit Wages and Salaries $95,000, credit Work-in-progress $95,000

   D   Debit Production Overheads $95,000, credit Work-in-progress $95,000

2 Which of the following is an example of a cost unit?

   A   Department 234

   B   A cost per labour hour in department 234

   C   Stationery costs in the administration department

   D   A service provided to a customer

3 A firm operates an integrated cost and financial accounting system.

   The accounting entries for an issue of direct materials to production would be:

   A   DR work-in-progress control account, CR stores control account

   B   DR finished goods account, CR stores control account

   C   DR stores control account, CR work-in-progress control account

   D   DR cost of sales account, CR work-in-progress control account.

4 During a period $35,750 was incurred for indirect labour. In a typical cost ledger, the double entry for this is:

   A   Dr Wages control $35,750   Cr Overhead control $35,750

   B   Dr WIP control $35,750   Cr Wages control $35,750

   C   Dr Overhead control $35,750   Cr Wages control $35,750

   D   Dr Wages control $35,750   Cr WIP control $35,750

5 Which of the following is an example of computer hardware?

   A   Operating system

   B   Spreadsheet package

   C   Modem

   D   Graphical user interface

For the answers to these questions, see the 'Answers' section at the end of the book.

Chapter 3

COST CLASSIFICATION AND COST BEHAVIOUR

This chapter explains that costs can be classified in different ways, according to the purpose for which the cost information is required. Several different methods of classifying costs are described. The chapter then goes on to explain that one important method of classifying costs is according to how the amount of the cost varies as the volume of output or level of activity changes. This is classifying costs according to 'cost behaviour'. Where possible, costs are classified by behaviour into either fixed or variable costs, and one technique that needs to be learned for identifying fixed and variable cost elements is the high-low method. This chapter covers syllabus area A3.

CONTENTS

1 Classification of costs

2 Cost behaviour

3 Estimating future costs with cost behaviour analysis

4 High-low method

LEARNING OUTCOMES

At the end of this chapter you should be able to:

- describe the variety of cost classifications used for different purposes in a cost accounting system, including by responsibility, function, direct/indirect, behaviour

- explain and illustrate the nature of variable, fixed and mixed (semi-variable, stepped-fixed) costs

- use the high-low method to separate semi-variable costs

- use variable, fixed and semi-variable costs in cost analysis

- analyse the effect of changing activity levels on unit costs.

1 CLASSIFICATION OF COSTS

Cost classification is the analysis of costs into logical groups so that they may be summarised into meaningful information for management.

Costs can be classified in different ways, according to the purpose for which they are to be used. Some of the methods of classifying costs are to separate them into:

- functional costs
- expense type, such as materials costs, labour costs and other expenses
- direct and indirect costs (overheads)
- fixed and variable costs, that is analysis by cost behaviour.

1.1 FUNCTIONAL ANALYSIS OF COSTS

In cost accounting, costs are often analysed by function, and categories of functional costs commonly used are:

- manufacturing costs
- administration costs
- selling and distribution costs (or marketing costs)
- possibly, research and development costs.

The functions used for costing will depend on the type of organisation. For example, there are no manufacturing costs in a service business. The reasons for classifying costs by function might be to:

- produce an income statement
- decide which costs should or should not be used to value inventory
- apply cost control. Costs of each function can be compared with a budget and the manager responsible for those costs held accountable for any inefficient or wasteful spending. For example, the production manager will be held responsible for production costs and the sales manager for selling costs.

1.2 MATERIALS, LABOUR AND EXPENSES

Another basic classification of costs widely used in cost accounting is to distinguish between the cost of materials, such as raw materials or components, the cost of labour and other expenses. We shall look at materials, labour and expenses in more detail in the following chapters.

COST CLASSIFICATION AND COST BEHAVIOUR : CHAPTER 3

1.3 DIRECT AND INDIRECT COSTS, PRIME COST AND OVERHEADS

The classification of costs into direct and indirect costs is a very important technique which is used to build up the full cost of a cost unit. A cost unit may be a product or service, a job or a contract. Cost units may be produced in batches or through a series of processes, in which case the full cost of the batch or process is collected and the cost per cost unit is found by dividing by the number of units of output.

- A **direct cost** is expenditure that can be directly identified with a specific cost unit. For example, direct material costs in a product are the costs of the materials that go into making that product. Direct labour costs of a product are the costs of the labour engaged directly in the manufacture of the product. Direct expenses are not so common for products, but the cost of a job or a contract could include the direct expenses of equipment hired to do the work or the direct cost of sub-contractors.

    Some costs may, technically, be direct costs but be so small in value that it is not economical to trace the expenditure to the cost unit. For example, the cost of sewing thread when making clothes, the cost of nails for a building job. These costs may be classified as indirect costs because the cost of recording them exceeds the value of the increased accuracy that would be gained.

- **Prime cost** is the total of direct materials cost, direct labour cost and direct expenses.

- **Indirect costs** or **overheads** are expenditure which cannot be directly identified with a specific cost unit and must be 'shared out' on an equitable basis. For example in a manufacturing company, the cost of indirect materials include the cost of materials used to clean and maintain machinery. Indirect labour costs of a product are the costs of labour that does not spend a measurable amount of time directly on making the product. Indirect expenses usually include all general expenses, such as the costs of building rental, heating and lighting and so on.

The **total production cost** or **full factory cost** of a cost unit is its prime cost or direct cost, plus its share of production overheads, consisting of indirect materials, indirect labour and indirect expenses.

The methods used to attribute a share of overhead costs to cost units is explained in a later chapter.

Summary

	$
Direct materials	X
Direct labour	X
Direct expenses (occasionally)	X
Prime cost	X
Production overhead	X
Full factory cost	X

Note: In a business there will also be non-manufacturing overheads such as administration and selling and distribution.

KAPLAN PUBLISHING 43

MA 2 : MANAGING COSTS AND FINANCES

ACTIVITY 1

Classify

A company manufactures and retails clothing. Group the costs (1) – (10) below into the classifications (i) to (viii) (each cost is intended to belong to only one classification).

Costs

(1) lubricant for sewing machines

(2) floppy disks for general office computer

(3) wages of operatives in the cutting department

(4) telephone rental plus metered calls

(5) interest on bank overdraft

(6) performing rights society charge for music broadcast throughout the factory

(7) market research undertaken prior to a new product launch

(8) wages of security guards for factory

(9) carriage on purchases of basic raw material

(10) royalty payable on number of units of product XY produced

Classifications

(i) direct materials

(ii) direct labour

(iii) direct expenses

(iv) production overhead

(v) research and development costs

(vi) selling and distribution costs

(vii) administration costs

(viii) finance costs

For a suggested answer, see the 'Answers' section at the end of the book.

COST CLASSIFICATION AND COST BEHAVIOUR : CHAPTER 3

2 COST BEHAVIOUR

Cost behaviour means the way that a cost changes as the volume of activity or output rises. For example, if a company manufactures widgets, we would expect the total cost of making and selling 10,000 widgets to be more than the total cost of making and selling 5,000 widgets. In other words, total costs should rise as the volume of output and sales rises.

However, not all individual items of expense will incur higher costs as the output level rises and if they do it may not be in direct proportion.

Cost behaviour analysis is concerned with how costs change with the 'level of activity' and by how much. Individual items of cost can be classified according to their cost behaviour. There are many different cost behaviour 'patterns', but many costs can be classified according to behaviour as:

- fixed costs
- variable costs
- semi-variable (and semi-fixed) costs
- stepped-fixed costs.

2.1 FIXED COSTS

Definition   **Fixed costs** are costs that are not affected in total by the level of activity, but remain the same amount regardless of how much or how little work is done in a period.

An example is the rent of a factory, which is a constant amount each period regardless of how much or how little is manufactured inside it.

The rent paid on a factory may be $5,000 per month whether 2 widgets or 200 widgets are made, as in the diagram below.

Fixed costs in total

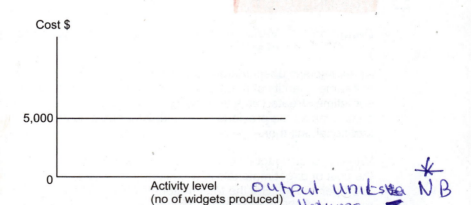

In reality, there must be a level of activity so large that more than one factory must be rented and rent is no longer a fixed cost (but a stepped-fixed cost). However, as long as we are only considering a reasonable range of activity, rent can be considered to be a fixed cost. This reasonable range of activity is known as the **relevant range**. If an organisation's normal output is within the relevant range, then rent can be considered to be a fixed cost.

MA 2 : MANAGING COSTS AND FINANCES

Note that a fixed cost is not a cost that necessarily stays the same over a period of time. The key is that it doesn't vary with activity. So, for example, heating costs are generally considered to be fixed as they must be paid regardless of the level of production. These costs will be higher in winter than in summer.

If an item of cost is fixed in total, then the cost per unit must fall as the activity level increases, as in the diagram that follows.

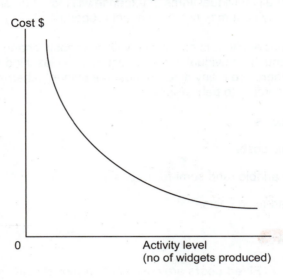

Fixed cost per unit

If 2 widgets are made the fixed cost per unit is $\frac{\$5,000}{2}$, i.e. $2,500 per widget.

If 200 widgets are made the fixed cost per unit is $\frac{\$5,000}{200}$, i.e. $25 per widget.

Conclusion   As the activity level increases, fixed costs remain the same in total, but the cost per unit of activity falls.

2.2 VARIABLE COSTS

Definition   **Variable costs** are costs that change in direct proportion to the level of activity.

An example is direct materials costs. Each additional unit produced of a product needs the same quantity of materials, which costs the same. Similarly, direct labour is sometimes treated as a variable cost, because each extra unit produced needs the same time as the previous units and, if labour is costed on a time basis, each additional unit therefore costs the same in labour.

Variable costs in total change at the same rate as the level of activity. For example, if the cost of direct materials is two kilograms at $2 per kg for each widget, this amounts to $4 per widget. So, the total materials cost is $4 if one unit is made, $8 if 2 units are made and $800 if 200 units are made, as in the diagram below.

Variable costs in total

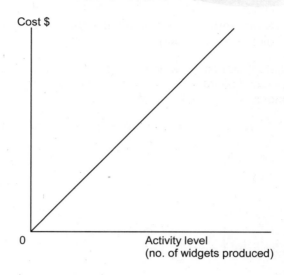

In practice, as the activity level increases, there might be changes in the additional cost of each unit. For example, as an organisation buys ever greater quantities of materials, it might be able to negotiate a bulk discount from its suppliers, so that the materials cost per unit of product falls. However, within a reasonable range of activity levels, it is often found that the variable cost per unit of output remains much the same. This is illustrated in the diagram below.

Variable cost per unit

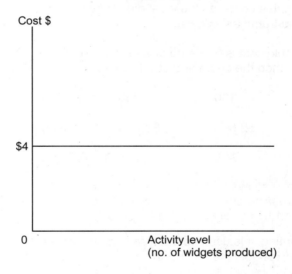

Conclusion   As the level of activity increases, total variable costs increase in direct proportion to the increase in activity, but the variable cost per unit of activity remains the same.

2.3 SEMI-VARIABLE COSTS

Definition   **Semi-variable costs** are those that have both fixed and variable elements.

An example is telephone costs, which consist of a fixed period rental and charges for calls made. Since call charges tend to vary with the volume of activity, telephone charges are roughly semi-variable in relation to the volume of production and sales.

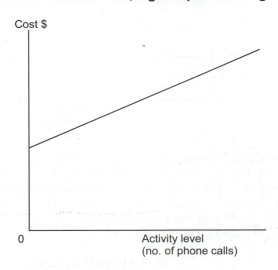

A semi-variable cost, e.g. telephone charges

With semi-variable costs, as the level of activity increases the cost per unit falls. This can be demonstrated as follows.

If a semi-variable cost is made up of a fixed element of $2,000 and a variable element of $5 per unit, then the cost per unit will fall as the activity level rises as follows:

Activity level	100	200	300	400
Total cost	$2,500	$3,000	$3,500	$4,000
Cost per unit	$25	$15	$11.67	$10

The table above shows that the rate at which the cost per unit falls as the activity level rises is a decreasing one i.e. it falls from $25 to $15 (a $10 fall per 100 units) then from $15 to $11.67 (a fall of $3.33 per 100 units) and so on.

In cost accounting, it is usual to analyse semi-variable costs by separating them into their fixed and variable elements. An important technique for doing this is the high-low method, which is described later.

2.4 STEPPED-FIXED COSTS

Definition   **Stepped-fixed costs**, also called **step** costs, are costs that are constant for a range of activity levels, and then change, and are constant again for another range.

An example is the cost of supervisors' salaries. For example, for production of up to 50 widgets, it might be sufficient to have just one supervisor, whereas if 50 to 100 are made two supervisors would be necessary and so on.

The key feature of stepped-fixed costs is that they are fixed within a limited range of activity, but then go up a step as the activity level rises beyond a certain level.

COST CLASSIFICATION AND COST BEHAVIOUR : CHAPTER 3

Stepped-fixed costs, e.g. supervisors' salaries

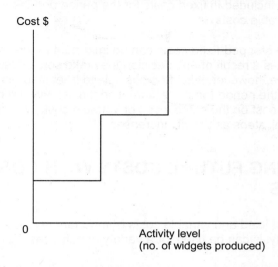

The stepped-fixed cost per unit is not constant and as the level of activity increases within a given range of activity the stepped-fixed cost per unit falls. This is very similar to the way in which the fixed cost per unit falls as activity levels increase. The main difference is that each time the fixed cost goes up in a 'step' the fixed cost per unit will be at its highest and then as the level of activity increases in the given range, the stepped-fixed cost per unit will fall until the cost goes up in another 'step' again. This can be demonstrated in the table shown below for a stepped-fixed cost that increases by $5,000 as the activity level increase by 100 units.

Activity level in units (range)	0–100	101–200	201–300	301–400
Stepped-fixed cost	$5,000	$10,000	$15,000	$20,000
Cost per unit	1 unit = $5,000 50 units = $100 100 units = $50	101 units = $99 150 units = $67 200 units = $50	201 units = $75 250 units = $60 300 units = $50	301 units = $66.5 350 units = $57 400 units = $50

2.5 USING FIXED AND VARIABLE COSTS

The distinction between fixed and variable costs might be used:

- in product costing (for example in marginal costing, which is explained later)
- to help to analyse profitability
- to help managers to make decisions about increasing or decreasing activity levels
- to estimate future costs (forecasting and budgeting)
- to estimate what costs should have been (for budgetary control) and performance assessment.

MA 2 : MANAGING COSTS AND FINANCES

Semi-variable costs are usually divided into their fixed and variable components. The fixed portion is included in fixed costs for the period and the variable portion included within total variable costs.

Knowing about stepped-fixed costs can be important for decision-makers, who need to know whether as a result of any decision they take some costs might rise or fall a step. In practice, however, it is often possible to treat stepped-fixed costs as either fixed costs for the period (on the assumption that activity will remain within a range that keeps the cost on the same level) or variable costs, where there are a large number of small steps as activity increases.

3 ESTIMATING FUTURE COSTS WITH COST BEHAVIOUR ANALYSIS

A knowledge of fixed and variable costs is important in cost accounting, because cost behaviour analysis can be used for a variety of purposes. Two of these purposes are:

- estimating what future costs should be, given an estimated volume of activity, for example in budgeting

- comparing actual costs with the cost expected for the actual level of activity achieved (the flexed budget). This is a feature of control reports in cost accounting.

Example

A company manufactures two products, X and Y. The following costs have been estimated.

	Product X	Product Y
Direct materials cost per unit	$14	$12
Direct labour hours per unit	1.5 hours	2.5 hours
Direct labour cost per hour	$10	$10
Variable overhead costs per hour	$2	$2

Fixed costs for the period are expected to be $220,000, and it is expected that 5,000 units of Product X and 2,000 units of Product Y will be manufactured.

Required:

What are the total expected costs for the period?

Solution

	Product X 5,000 units $	Product Y 2,000 units $	Total $
Variable costs			
Direct materials	70,000	24,000	94,000
Direct labour	75,000	50,000	125,000
Variable overhead costs	15,000	10,000	25,000
Total variable costs	160,000	84,000	244,000
Fixed costs			220,000
Total costs			464,000

ACTIVITY 2

A business makes two products, C and D, with the following sales prices and cost data.

	C	D
Sales price per unit	$25	$30
Direct material cost per unit	$8	$7
Direct labour cost	$6 per unit	0.5 hours $8 per hour
Variable overhead	$1 per unit	$2 per direct labour hour

Fixed costs are $40,000 per month.

Given this information, what is the forecast of total costs and profits for a month when the business expects to make and sell 1,200 units of product C and 1,800 units of product D.

For a suggested answer, see the 'Answers' section at the end of the book.

Estimates of future costs may be shown as a cost function:

y = a + bx   where y = total cost

a = total fixed cost

b = variable cost per unit

x = number of units of output

If all but one piece of information is known this can be found by rearranging and solving the formula. The complete formula can then be used to forecast future costs.

Example

An organisation's cost function is known to be:

y = a + bx   where y = total cost

a = total fixed cost

b = variable cost per unit

x = number of units of output

The total cost for output of 1,000 units is $3,950 and the total variable cost is $1,350.

Required:

(i)   Calculate the fixed cost for the period.

(ii) Calculate the total cost if output were 1,250 units.

(iii) Calculate the cost per unit if output were 900 units.

Solution

(i)   Total cost = fixed cost + variable cost

$3,950 = fixed cost + $1,350

Therefore fixed cost = $3,950 − $1,350 = $2,600

(ii) The variable cost per unit = $1,350 /1,000 = $1.35 per unit

The cost function is:

y = 2,600 + 1.35x

If x = 1,250 then total cost = 2,600 + (1.35 × 1,250) = $4,287.50

(iii) If x = 900 then total cost = 2,600 + (1.35 × 900) = $3,815

The cost per unit = $3,815/900 = $4.24 (to 2 d.p.)

4 HIGH-LOW METHOD

The high-low method estimates fixed and variable costs by comparing the costs of the highest and lowest activity levels and analysing the difference between them.

- We take the cost information for the highest activity level and for the lowest activity level, from the data available. The assumption is that the total cost line goes through these two points.

- Assuming that fixed costs are the same at both activity levels, the difference in total cost between the highest and the lowest activity levels must be attributable to variable costs entirely. The difference must be the variable cost for the number of units of activity between the lowest and the highest points.

- This allows us to calculate a variable cost per unit. Having done this, we can apply the variable cost value to either the low cost or the high cost data, to calculate the fixed costs.

This method of analysis is based on historical data for costs at different activity levels. If there has been inflation in costs over the time periods covered by this data, all the costs should be re-stated at a common price level.

To illustrate the high-low method, the data below will be used as an example.

Example

Inspection costs for the six months to 31 December 20X8 are as follows:

Month	Units produced	Cost $
July	340	2,260
August	300	2,160
September	380	2,320
October	420	2,400
November	400	2,300
December	360	2,266

Required:

Use the high-low method to calculate the fixed costs per month and the variable cost per unit.

Solution

The variable element of a cost item may be estimated by calculating the unit cost between high and low volumes during a period.

Note: Take the highest and lowest **activity volumes**. These might not be the highest or lowest costs.

High month = October (420). Low month = August (300).

	Units	Total cost
		$
High	420	2,400
Low	300	2,160
	120	240

Variable cost per unit = $240/120 = $2.

Having calculated the variable cost per unit, we can calculate the fixed costs from either the high or the low activity level costs.

420 units	$
Total cost	2,400
Less: Variable cost (420 × $2)	840
Therefore fixed cost	1,560

Inspection costs are therefore estimated as $1,560 per month plus $2 per unit produced.

Advantages and limitations of the high-low method

The high-low method has the enormous advantage of simplicity. It is easy to understand and easy to use.

The limitations of the high-low method are as follows.

- It relies on historical data, assuming that (i) activity is the only factor affecting costs and (ii) historical costs reliably predict future costs.

- It uses only two values, the highest and the lowest, which means that the results may be distorted because of random variations in these values.

MA 2 : MANAGING COSTS AND FINANCES

ACTIVITY 3

Use the high-low method to calculate the fixed and variable elements of the following costs:

	Activity	$
January	400	1,050
February	600	1,700
March	550	1,600
April	800	2,100
May	750	2,000
June	900	2,300

For a suggested answer, see the 'Answers' section at the end of the book.

CONCLUSION

Accurate classification of costs is often an important first step in cost accounting techniques. The use of direct/indirect costs and knowledge of cost behaviour is fundamental to the syllabus and you should learn the definitions carefully and be prepared to use them.

KEY TERMS

Direct cost – expenditure which can be directly identified with a specific cost unit or cost centre.

Prime cost – the aggregate of direct materials cost, direct labour cost and direct expenses.

Indirect costs – expenditure which cannot be directly identified with a specific cost unit or cost centre. Also called **overheads**.

Cost behaviour – how costs vary as the level of activity (e.g. output or sales) varies.

Fixed costs – costs which are not affected in total by the level of activity.

Variable costs – costs which change in total in direct proportion to the level of activity.

Semi-variable costs – costs which have both fixed and variable elements.

Stepped-fixed costs – costs which are constant for a range of activity levels, and then change and are constant again for another range. Also called step costs.

COST CLASSIFICATION AND COST BEHAVIOUR : CHAPTER 3

SELF TEST QUESTIONS

Paragraph

1   Define a direct cost.   1.3

2   What is a prime cost?   1.3

3   Give an example of an indirect cost.   1.3

4   Sketch a graph of total fixed cost.   2.1

5   What is the relevant range?   2.1

6   Sketch a graph of total variable cost.   2.2

7   Explain how the high-low method is used.   4

EXAM-STYLE QUESTIONS

1   Which is NOT an example of a functional analysis of costs?

   A   Overheads

   B   Marketing costs

   C   Selling costs

   D   Manufacturing costs

2   Which of the following would be classed as indirect labour?

   A   Assembly workers

   B   A stores assistant in a factory store

   C   Plasterers in a building company

   D   An audit clerk in an accountancy firm

3   Direct costs are:

   A   costs that can always be identified with a single cost unit

   B   costs that can be identified with a single cost unit or a batch of cost units

   C   costs that can be attributed to an accounting period

   D   costs that change in direct proportion to the number of units produced

KAPLAN PUBLISHING

4 A firm is trying to find a relationship between its sales volume in a quarter and its telephone expense that quarter.

If a sales volume of 2 million units corresponds to a telephone expense of $5,000 and sales volume of 4 million units corresponds to a telephone expense of $6,000, then if the sales volume is 5 million units, the telephone expense is likely to be:

A $2,500

B $6,500

C $7,000

D $7,500

5 Which of the following graphs depicts the cost per unit of fixed cost?

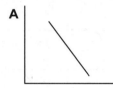

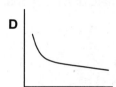

6 The following data are records of output levels and overhead costs.

	January	December
Hours worked	18,000	21,000
Total costs	$86,800	$97,438

There was 3% inflation between January and December. The variable cost per hour worked, at January price levels and to the nearest $0.01, is:

A $4.52

B $2.68

C $3.55

D $2.60

7 The 'high-low' method of cost estimation can be used to:

A calculate the forecast cost for a given volume of activity

B calculate the highest and lowest cost in the period

C measure the actual cost of an activity

D predict the range of costs expected in a period

COST CLASSIFICATION AND COST BEHAVIOUR : CHAPTER 3

8   The following information relates to the overhead costs of the production department:

Units of output	5,000	7,000
Overheads	$21,100	$26,100

The variable overhead rate per unit is $2.50. The amount of fixed overhead is:

A $5,000

B $8,600

C $13,600

D $21,100

The following information relates to questions 9 and 10

Bronze recorded the following costs for the past six months.

Month	Activity level Units	Total cost $
1	80	6,586
2	60	5,826
3	72	6,282
4	75	6,396
5	83	6,700
6	66	6,054

9   The estimated fixed costs per month are:

A $4,422

B $3,546

C $2,654

D $5,186

10 The estimated total costs of producing 90 units would be:

A $6,966

B $6,844

C $7,222

D $6,886

For the answers to these questions, see the 'Answers' section at the end of the book.

MA 2 : MANAGING COSTS AND FINANCES

Chapter 4

ACCOUNTING FOR MATERIALS

This chapter is the first of several that explain how the elements of cost are calculated and accounted for. The elements of cost are materials, labour and expenses. These can be either direct costs or indirect costs. This chapter covers syllabus area B1 (a) to (e).

CONTENTS

1. Direct and indirect materials
2. Procedures and documentation for materials
3. Pricing issues of materials
4. Accounting for materials costs
5. Inventory losses and waste

LEARNING OUTCOMES

At the end of this chapter you should be able to:

- describe the main types of material classification

- describe the procedures and documentation required to ensure the correct authorisation, coding, analysis and recording of direct and indirect material costs

- explain, illustrate and evaluate the FIFO, LIFO and periodic and cumulative weighted average methods used to price materials issued from inventory

- describe and illustrate the accounting for material costs

- calculate material input requirements, and control measures, where wastage occurs.

MA 2 : MANAGING COSTS AND FINANCES

1 DIRECT AND INDIRECT MATERIALS

In cost accounting, materials are commonly classified as either direct materials or indirect materials

Definition   **Direct materials** are the materials that can be directly attributed to a unit of production, or a specific job, or a service provided directly to a customer.

In a manufacturing business, direct materials are therefore the raw materials and components that are directly input into the products that the organisation makes. For example the many different components that make up a motorcar are the direct materials of the car.

Definition   **Indirect materials** are other materials that cannot be directly attributed to a unit of production.

An example of indirect materials might be the oil used for the lubrication of production machinery. This is a material that is used in the production process but it cannot be directly attributed to each unit of finished product.

In a manufacturing business, the **cost of direct materials** can be charged directly to the cost unit that uses the materials. In a jobbing business or a contracting business, direct materials costs are charged directly to the job or contract for which they are used.

The **costs of indirect materials** are charged to the cost centre that requisitions them from the stores department and uses them.

2 PROCEDURES AND DOCUMENTATION FOR MATERIALS

The stores department is responsible for the receipt, storage and issue of materials and components.

- **Receipt of materials into store**. When materials are received from suppliers, they are normally delivered to the stores department. The stores personnel must check that the goods delivered are the ones that have been ordered, in the correct quantity, of the correct quality and in good condition.

- Once the materials have been received they must be **stored** until required by user departments.

- **Issue of materials from store**. When cost centres require materials, they submit a requisition for the materials to the stores department.

- **Recording receipts and issues**. Receipts of materials into store and issues of materials must be controlled and recorded. Oddly perhaps, the responsibility for recording receipts and issues of materials is divided between the stores department and the costing department. Each of these departments could maintain its own separate inventory records, although there should ideally be one integrated inventory control system. The stores department should monitor the quantities of materials received and issued, and ensure the safety and security of the physical inventory. The costing department is responsible for recording the cost of materials received into stores and for putting a value to the cost of direct and indirect materials issued from store.

2.1 PROCEDURES AND DOCUMENTATION FOR RECEIPTS OF MATERIALS

It is useful to have an overview of the departments involved in the purchasing process.

Stores department	Notifies the purchasing department of the need to buy materials, using a purchase requisition/inventory reorder form.
Purchasing department	Orders goods from external supplier using a purchase order.
External supplier	Delivers goods to the stores department. The goods are accompanied by a delivery note. The external supplier also sends a purchase invoice to the accounts department, asking for payment for the goods.
Stores department	Raises goods received note (GRN) from the delivery note details. The goods received note is used to update the inventory records with the quantities of goods received.
Costing department	The costing department records the cost of the materials received, using the delivery note and the purchase invoice details.

2.2 PROCEDURES AND DOCUMENTATION FOR THE ISSUE OF MATERIALS

Requests for materials to be issued from stores to a production department or other department are initiated and then authorised by a **materials requisition note**. This document performs two functions: it authorises the storekeeper to release the goods and acts as a source record for updating the stores records.

An example of a materials requisition document is shown below.

MATERIAL REQUISITION

Serial No: ....

Charge Job/
Cost Centre No: ....

Date: ....

Code No.	Description	Quantity or weight	Cost office only				
			Rate	Unit	$	$	Stores ledger

Authorised by:	Storekeeper:	Price entered by:
Received by:	Bin card entered:	Calculations checked:

MA 2 : MANAGING COSTS AND FINANCES

Notes:

1. Every item of inventory has a unique identity code. The materials requisition note is filled in to show both the code and the description of the materials requisitioned.

2. The materials requisition note also identifies the job or cost centre for which the materials are issued.

3. The materials issued from stores must be given a price or value. The task of pricing materials issued from stores is the responsibility of the costing department. A copy of the requisition is sent to the costing department, which calculates and enters the costs.

2.3 STORES RECORDS

In any inventory control system, there should be a continual record of the current quantities of each item of inventory held in store. Receipts into store and issues from store must be recorded, so that the current inventory balance can be kept up-to-date.

When the stores control system is a paper-based system, there could be two separate inventory records:

- a **bin card system**, in which a stores record (a 'bin card') is kept for each item of inventory. The bin card is held in the stores department, and is used to record the **quantities only** of inventory received and issued and the current inventory balance

- an **inventory ledger system**, in which a record is kept for the cost ledger for each item of inventory. In a paper-based system, there is a stores ledger card for each item of inventory. This is kept up-to-date by the costing department, and **records both the quantity and value** of items received into stores, issued from stores and the current balance held in stores.

STORES LEDGER CARD

Description .... Unit .... Location .... Code ....
Maximum .... Minimum .... Reorder level .... Reorder quantity ....

Receipts			Issues				On order		
Date/ ref	Quantity	$	Date/ ref	Quantity	$	Physical balance	Date/ ref	Quantity	$

Note:

The purchase cost of materials excludes any Sales Tax. It includes any costs associated with buying the materials that the business is required to pay, notably the costs of freight and delivery ('carriage inwards' costs).

When an inventory **control system is computerised**, there will be just one stores ledger record system. For each item of inventory, there is a computer record similar to a stores ledger card, showing both the quantities and the value of items received and issued, and the current inventory balance.

3 PRICING ISSUES OF MATERIALS

When materials are purchased, the process of giving them a value is fairly straightforward. The purchase cost of the items is the price charged by the supplier (excluding any Sales Tax) plus any carriage inwards costs. The cost should be net of any trade discount given.

When materials are issued from store, a cost or price has to be attached to them.

- When a quantity of materials is purchased in its entirety for a specific job, the purchase cost can be charged directly to the job.

- More commonly however, materials are purchased in fairly large quantities (but at different prices each time) and later issued to cost centres in smaller quantities. It would be administratively extremely difficult, if not impossible, to identify specific units of material that have been purchased with units issued to cost centres. Consequently, when issues of materials from store are being valued/priced, we do not try to identify what the specific units actually did cost. Instead, materials issued from store are valued/priced on the basis of a valuation method.

A business might use any of several valuation methods for pricing stores issued. Three such methods are:

- First in first out (FIFO)
- Last in first out (LIFO)
- Weighted average cost (AVCO).

Example

The same example will be used to illustrate each of these methods.

In November 1,000 tonnes of inventory item 1234 were purchased in three lots:

3 November	400 tonnes at $60 per tonne
11 November	300 tonnes at $70 per tonne
21 November	300 tonnes at $80 per tonne

During the same period four materials requisitions were completed for 200 tonnes each, on 5, 14, 22 and 27 November.

3.1 FIRST IN FIRST OUT (FIFO) METHOD

With the first in first out method of valuation, it is assumed that materials are issued from store in the order in which they were received. In the example above, it would be assumed with FIFO that the 400 tonnes purchased at $60 each on 3 November will be used before the 300 tonnes bought on 11 November, and these in turn will be used before the 300 tonnes bought on 21 November.

The closing inventory at the end of November is 200 units. These consist of 200 of the most recently purchased units.

The stores ledger account for inventory item 1234 is summarised below.

Date	Receipts	Issues	Balance No.	$
3 Nov	400 × $60		400	24,000
5 Nov		200 × $60	200	12,000
11 Nov	300 × $70		500	33,000
14 Nov		200 × $60	300	21,000
21 Nov	300 × $80		600	45,000
22 Nov		200 × $70	400	31,000
27 Nov		100 × $70		
		100 × $80	200	16,000

Note that each successive consignment into stores is exhausted before charging issues from stores at the next price.

Using this method the total value of materials issued is $53,000 and the value of closing inventory is $16,000.

3.2 LAST IN FIRST OUT (LIFO) METHOD

With the last in first out method of pricing, it is assumed that materials issued from stores are the units that were acquired the most recently of those still remaining in inventory.

In this example, the 200 tonnes issued on 5 November will therefore consist of materials purchased on 3 November, the 200 tonnes issued on 14 November will consist of materials purchased on 11 November and the 200 tonnes issued on 22 November will consist of materials purchased on 21 November. The materials issued on 27 November will consist of the remaining 100 tonnes bought on 21 November and the 100 tonnes bought on 14 November.

The closing inventory at the end of November consists of 200 of the tonnes bought on 5 November.

The stores ledger card for item 1234 using LIFO would be as follows.

Date	Receipts	Issues	Balance No.	$
3 Nov	400 × $60		400	24,000
5 Nov		200 × $60	200	12,000
11 Nov	300 × $70		500	33,000
14 Nov		200 × $70	300	19,000
21 Nov	300 × $80		600	43,000
22 Nov		200 × $80	400	27,000
27 Nov		100 × $80		
		100 × $70	200	12,000

Using this method the total value of materials issued is $57,000 (more than under FIFO) and the closing inventory value is $12,000 (less than FIFO). When prices are rising this will always be the case.

3.3 WEIGHTED AVERAGE COST (AVCO) METHOD

With the weighted average cost method of pricing material issues, all quantities of an item of inventory are valued at a weighted average cost. A new weighted average cost is calculated each time that there is a new delivery into stores. A weighted average price is usually calculated to the nearest cent.

Weighted average price = $\dfrac{\text{Inventory value of items in stores} + \text{Purchase cost of units received}}{\text{Quantity already in stores} + \text{Quantity received}}$

The price so calculated is used to value all subsequent issues until the next consignment of the inventory is received into stores and a new weighted average cost is calculated.

		Item 1234		
		Receipts (issues)		Weighted average price
Date	Quantity	Purchase price	Value	(issue price)
		$	$	$
3 Nov	400	60	24,000	60
5 Nov	(200)		(12,000)	60
	200		12,000	60
11 Nov	300	70	21,000	
Balance	500		33,000	66 (W1)
14 Nov	(200)		(13,200)	66
	300		19,800	66
21 Nov	300	80	24,000	
Balance	600		43,800	73 (W2)
22 Nov	(200)		(14,600)	73
27 Nov	(200)		(14,600)	73
30 Nov (bal)	200		14,600	73

A new average cost price calculation is required after each new receipt.

Workings

(W1) $33,000/500 = $66

(W2) $43,800/600 = $73

Using this method the total value of materials issued is $54,400 and the closing inventory value is $14,600. These figures are between the FIFO and LIFO valuations.

A variation on the AVCO method is the **periodic** weighted average cost method.

3.4 PERIODIC WEIGHTED AVERAGE COST METHOD

With the periodic weighted average cost method of pricing inventory an average price is calculated at the end of the period which is then used to price all issues.

Periodic weighted average price =

$\dfrac{\text{Cost of opening inventory} + \text{Cost of all receipts in the period}}{\text{Units in opening inventory} + \text{Units received}}$

The stores ledger card for the item 1234 would be as follows:

Item 1234
Receipts (Issues)

Date	Quantity	Purchase price	Value	Periodic Weighted Average price (issue price)
3 Nov	400	60	24,000	
11 Nov	300	70	21,000	
21 Nov	300	80	24,000	
	1,000		69,000	69.00
5 Nov	(200)		(13,800)	69.00
14 Nov	(200)		(13,800)	69.00
22 Nov	(200)		(13,800)	69.00
27 Nov	(200)		(13,800)	69.00
30 Nov (bal)	200		13,800	69.00

Using this method the total value of materials issued is $55,200 and the closing inventory value is $13,800. Note that using this method the cost of issues cannot be calculated until the end of the period.

ACTIVITY 1

You are given the following information about one line of inventory held by Tolley plc.

Assuming that there are no further transactions in the month of May, what is the value of the issues made on 1 March and 1 May and what would be the inventory valuation, using (i) the FIFO valuation method (ii) LIFO and (iii) AVCO (iv) Periodic weighted average pricing?

How does the inventory pricing method used impact on the profit made on sales?

		Units	Cost $	Sales price $
Opening inventory	1 January	50	7	
Purchase	1 February	60	8	
Sale	1 March	40		10
Purchase	1 April	70	9	
Sale	1 May	60		12

For a suggested answer, see the 'Answers' section at the end of the book.

3.5 COMPARISON OF VALUATION METHODS – THE EFFECT ON PROFIT OF THE INVENTORY VALUATION METHOD SELECTED

A business can choose whichever method of inventory valuation it wants to use. FIFO and weighted average costs are both acceptable for financial reporting, whereas LIFO is not. However, in cost accounting, the rules of financial reporting do not apply, and businesses can use LIFO should they wish.

If the purchase price of materials stayed the same indefinitely, every inventory valuation method would produce the same values for stores issues and closing inventory. Differences between the valuation methods is usually only significant during a period of price inflation, because the choice of valuation method can have a significant effect on the value of materials consumed (and so on the cost of sales and profits) and on closing inventory values.

The relative advantages and disadvantages of FIFO, LIFO and AVCO are therefore discussed below, particularly in relation to **inflationary situations**.

Method	Advantages	Disadvantages
FIFO	• Produces current values for closing inventory.	• Produces out-of-date production costs and therefore potentially overstates profits. • Complicates inventory records as inventory must be analysed by delivery.
LIFO	• Produces realistic production costs and therefore more realistic/prudent profit figures.	• Produces unrealistically low closing inventory values. • Complicates inventory records as inventory must be analysed by delivery.
Weighted average price	• Simple to operate – calculations within the inventory records are minimised.	• Produces both inventory values and production costs which are likely to differ from current values.

Whichever method is adopted it should be applied consistently from period to period.

4 ACCOUNTING FOR MATERIALS COSTS

Within the inventory control system, there is an inventory ledger account for each item held in stores.

This inventory ledger account records details of all receipts of the material as well as all issues of the material to production.

The information in a stores ledger account can be presented in the form of a T account, for double entry bookkeeping purposes, as follows.

Inventory ledger account – item 2345

	$		$
Opening balance b/d	X	Issues	X
Receipts	X	Closing balance c/d	X
	—		—
Balance b/d	X		X
	—		—
	X		

There is an account for each item of inventory in the inventory control system, but in the cost ledger accounting system, there is an **inventory control account** for all items of inventory in total. In other words, the materials cost ledger account shows in total all of the entries that have taken place in the individual inventory ledger accounts. The materials cost ledger account therefore records the total materials purchases for the organisation, and the total value of materials issued to production as direct materials or to cost centres as indirect materials.

MA 2 : MANAGING COSTS AND FINANCES

4.1 PURCHASE OF MATERIALS

When materials are purchased and the purchases are recorded in the cost accounts, the credit side of the entry will be to either cash (cash purchases) or creditors (credit purchases). The debit entry is in the stores account, recording the purchase cost of the materials.

Example

Ogden Ltd is a small company that was set up at the beginning of May 20X4 by the issue of $20,000 of shares for cash. Ogden Ltd purchases three types of material: A, B and C. During the month of May 20X4 the purchases of each type of material were as follows:

Material A

| 3 May | $2,000 |
| 24 May | $9,000 |

Material B

6 May	$5,000
10 May	$3,000
21 May	$7,000

Material C

1 May	$4,000
7 May	$4,000
28 May	$4,000

Purchases of materials A and B are for cash and material C is on credit of 45 days.

Record these transactions in the individual inventory ledger accounts as well as the cash and creditor accounts.

Solution

Inventory ledger account Material A

	$		$
3 May	2,000		
24 May	9,000		

Inventory ledger account Material B

	$		$
6 May	5,000		
10 May	3,000		
21 May	7,000		

Inventory ledger account Material C

	$		$
1 May	4,000		
7 May	4,000		
28 May	4,000		

ACCOUNTING FOR MATERIALS : CHAPTER 4

Cash account

		$		$
1 May	Share capital a/c	20,000	3 May Material A	2,000
			6 May Material B	5,000
			10 May Material B	3,000
			21 May Material B	7,000
			24 May Material A	9,000

Payables account

	$		$
		1 May Material C	4,000
		7 May Material C	4,000
		28 May Material C	4,000

Note: The inventory control account would include all of the entries for Materials A, B and C.

4.2 ISSUES OF MATERIALS

Materials issued from stores are recorded as a credit entry in the stores account. The value or cost of the materials issued is determined by whichever valuation method is used (FIFO, LIFO, weighted average cost, etc).

The corresponding double entry is to:

- a work-in-progress account, for direct materials

- an overhead account, for indirect materials. (This can be a production overhead, administration overhead or selling and distribution overhead, according to the function of the cost centre that obtains the materials.)

Continuing the example from paragraph 4.1, now suppose that Ogden Ltd made the following issues of materials in June:

Material A	Direct material to production	$7,000
Material B	To selling and distribution	$3,000
	To administration	$4,000
Material C	Indirect material to production	$3,000

The ledger accounts would be completed as follows.

Inventory ledger control account

	$		$
Opening balance	38,000	WIP (Material A)	7,000
		Selling and distribution overhead (Material B)	3,000
		Administration overhead (Material B)	4,000
		Production overhead (Material C)	3,000
		Closing balance (bal. fig.)	21,000
	38,000		38,000

KAPLAN PUBLISHING

69

Work-in-progress (WIP)

	$		$
Stores control	7,000		

Production overhead control

	$		$
Stores control	3,000		

Administration overhead

	$		$
Stores control	4,000		

Selling and distribution overhead

	$		$
Stores control	3,000		

5 INVENTORY LOSSES AND WASTE

5.1 MATERIAL INPUT REQUIREMENTS

In some manufacturing processes, there is wastage or loss of inventory. When wastage is expected during processing, the department using the materials should allow for the losses when it orders materials.

Wastage is usually measured as a percentage of the quantities of materials input.

Input – Wastage = Output

For example, if wastage is 3% of input, output will be 97% of input. In formula terms:

$$\text{Input} = \text{Output} \times \frac{100\%}{(100\% - \text{wastage rate percentage})}$$

So if the required output is 500 units, the input material requirements are:

$$\text{Input} = 500 \text{ units} \times \frac{100}{(100 - 3)}$$

= 515.5 units, say 516 units.

ACTIVITY 2

In a production process, there is usually a wastage rate of 5% of input. Materials cost $8 per kilogram. The required output is 1,520 kilograms.

Required:

What quantity of input materials should be required, and what will they cost?

For a suggested answer, see the 'Answers' section at the end of the book.

5.2 CONTROL MEASURES

If wastage is a normal part of the production process, control measures should be calculated and actual wastage rates compared to the control measures to check that the wastage rates are as expected. If wastage is greater or less than expected, the reasons why this has happened must be investigated and action taken as necessary.

Wastage may be greater than expected:

- if labour is less experienced than expected and make more mistakes when using the material

- if a machine is old or poorly maintained and there are more breakdowns and errors than expected

- if the production process has changed

- if the estimate of the control rate for wastage was too low.

Example

A business expects wastage to be 5% of material input. In a period actual material input was 250 kg and 230 kg of finished output was produced.

Compare the actual wastage rate with the expected wastage rate.

Solution

The actual wastage rate is 20/250 x 100% = 8%

This is higher than the expected wastage rate of 5% and the reasons for the difference should be investigated.

CONCLUSION

This chapter has explained in detail the procedures concerned with ordering, receiving, storing and issuing materials. It has illustrated the accounting techniques used to value materials. For your examination, it is important to have a working knowledge of the inventory valuation methods, particularly FIFO, LIFO and AVCO. You should also be able to compare these methods, particularly during a period of rising or falling prices.

KEY TERMS

Direct materials – materials that can be directly attributed to a unit of production, or a specific job or a service provided directly to a customer.

Indirect materials – materials that cannot be directly attributed to a unit of production.

FIFO – first in first out method of inventory valuation.

LIFO – last in first out method of inventory valuation.

AVCO – weighted average method of inventory valuation.

MA 2 : MANAGING COSTS AND FINANCES

SELF TEST QUESTIONS

		Paragraph
1	Distinguish between direct materials and indirect materials.	1
2	Which document is used to record materials issued from stores?	2.2
3	Under the LIFO method of inventory valuation at what price is closing inventory valued, the most recently or the earliest-purchased units of the item of inventory?	3.2
4	What are the advantages and disadvantages of the weighted average price method of inventory valuation?	3.5
5	What double entry is used to record the issue of materials from stores to a production overhead cost centre?	4.2
6	What formula can be used to calculate the required quantity of input materials, given a required output quantity and a wastage rate expressed as a percentage of input quantities?	5.1

EXAM-STYLE QUESTIONS

1   ABC Ltd had an opening inventory of $880 (275 units valued at $3.20 each) on 1 April.

The following receipts and issues were recorded during April:

8 April	receives 600 units at $3.00 each
15 April	receives 400 units at $3.40 each
30 April	issues 925 units

Possible inventory values:

- A $2,935
- B $4,040
- C $2,932
- D $2,850

(i)   What would be the value of the issues under LIFO?

(ii) What would be the total value of issues under AVCO?

(iii) What would the total value of issues under FIFO?

ACCOUNTING FOR MATERIALS : CHAPTER 4

2 W Ltd has closing inventory at 31 July of 400 units valued at $10,000 using LIFO. Inventory movements in July were:

5 July	300 units bought for $25/unit
10 July	500 units issued
15 July	400 units bought for $22/unit
20 July	200 units issued

What was the value of the opening inventory?

A $11,200

B $10,000

C $9,400

D Cannot be found

The following information relates to questions 3, 4, 5 and 6.

Inventory movements of component AB1 for the month of March were as follows:

8 March	4,000 received, total cost $20,000
15 March	3,900 issued
19 March	1,200 received, total cost $7,200
21 March	1,100 issued
24 March	2,800 received, total cost $21,000

3 What is the inventory valuation at 31 March on a LIFO basis?

A $22,100

B $22,500

C $15,000

D $18,000

4 What is the value of the issue made on 21 March using a FIFO basis?

A $6,600

B $5,500

C $8,250

D $6,500

KAPLAN PUBLISHING 73

MA 2 : MANAGING COSTS AND FINANCES

5 What is the inventory valuation at 31 March on a weighted average basis?

- A $18,075
- B $18,500
- C $22,185
- D $22,046

6 What is the value of the issue made on the 21 March on a weighted average basis?

- A $6,628
- B $6,515
- C $6,600
- D $6,570

7 A company uses FIFO inventory pricing and has a high level of inventory turnover. In a period of rising prices, the closing inventory valuation is:

- A close to current purchase prices
- B based on the prices of the first items received
- C much lower than current purchase prices
- D lower than if LIFO inventory pricing were used.

8 A and B are in business, buying and selling goods for resale. During September 20X3 the following transactions occurred:

September	1	Balance brought forward NIL
September	3	Bought 200 units at $1.00 each
September	7	Sold 180 units
September	8	Bought 240 units at $1.50 each
September	14	Sold 170 units
September	15	Bought 230 units at $2.00 each
September	21	Sold 150 units

The value of stock using the weighted average method of stock valuation to the nearest $) is:

- A $174
- B $285
- C $314
- D $340

For the answers to these questions, see the 'Answers' section at the end of the book.

Chapter 5

MATERIAL INVENTORY CONTROL

VERY NB for Exam

The previous chapter looked at how transactions involving direct and indirect materials are recorded and valued. This chapter looks at the control of inventory levels as a means of controlling the costs of stores administration. This chapter covers syllabus area B1 (f) to (j).

CONTENTS

1 Monitoring inventory and inventory losses

2 Costs of holding inventory and stockouts

3 Economic order quantity (EOQ)

4 Inventory re-order level

5 Materials costing and inventory control

LEARNING OUTCOMES

At the end of this chapter you should be able to:

- describe the procedures required to monitor inventory and to minimise inventory discrepancies and losses

- explain and illustrate the costs of holding inventory and of being without inventory

- explain, illustrate and evaluate inventory control levels (minimum, maximum, re-order)

- calculate and interpret optimal order quantities

- discuss the relationship between the materials costing system and the inventory control system.

1 MONITORING INVENTORY AND INVENTORY LOSSES

1.1 STOCKTAKING

Inventory records are kept on bin cards (in a manual stores control system) or in a computerised inventory control system. These record quantities purchased, quantities issued and the current balance held in inventory.

In practice, the records could become inaccurate. There are several reasons for this.

- There could be errors recording the quantities received or issued.

- A receipt into stores or an issue from stores might not be recorded at all, due to an oversight.

- Items of inventory might have to be thrown away, because they have deteriorated, and the write-off might not be recorded in the accounts.

- Inventory might get lost or stolen.

Inventory records should be kept as up-to-date as possible, and from time-to-time, there should be a physical count of the inventory actually held in store (a 'stocktake'). Actual quantities counted should be compared with the balances that should be in inventory, according to the records. Discrepancies should be investigated, and any errors in the accounts should be rectified.

Definition   A **stocktake** is the counting and recording of the physical quantities of each item of inventory.

Periodic stocktakes are carried out at a specified time, for example at the end of the accounting year. This can be very disruptive to production as it may involve closing the stores for several days. This approach also means that there are long periods between inventory checks and substantial discrepancies may build up.

Continuous stocktakes involve checking items on a rotating basis. All items are checked at least once a year but items which are of high value or are used frequently can be checked more often.

1.2 ACTION TO BE TAKEN

Once the reasons for the difference have been identified then the appropriate action must be taken.

- If errors have been made when writing up the bin card or items omitted then the bin card must be corrected.

- If items of inventory were stored in the wrong place then they must be moved and a new total of actual inventory held should be calculated.

- If items have been stolen then security arrangements must be reviewed and the cost of the items stolen accounted for as an expense of the business.

- If inventory is being lost because it has deteriorated and has to be thrown away, measures for improving storage conditions might be considered, in order to reduce losses.

2 COSTS OF HOLDING INVENTORY AND STOCKOUTS

Inventory is held so that sales can be made and profits can be earned. When inventory is held, a wider variety of products can be offered, customer demand can be satisfied immediately and production is not delayed waiting for a new delivery of raw materials. However, holding inventory can be expensive. The objective of an inventory policy should be to minimise the total annual costs associated with inventory.

The total costs associated with inventory include the following costs:

- purchase costs

- inventory holding costs

- inventory ordering costs

- stockouts (i.e. the costs of being without inventory when it is needed).

Holding inventory is expensive. Holding costs include interest on capital, the costs of storage space and equipment, administration costs, and losses from deterioration, pilferage and obsolescence. Holding costs can be reduced by keeping inventory levels to a minimum. This suggests that there ought to be a policy of purchasing materials in small-sized orders, which would have to be placed at frequent intervals.

Order costs are incurred every time inventory is purchased from a supplier. Order costs include the buyer's time spent contacting the supplier, and the storekeeper's time spent checking the goods received. Order costs can be reduced by placing orders only at infrequent intervals. However, this means that order quantities need to be large, to reduce the total overall order costs for the year. Such a policy would result in high average levels of inventory, which increases holding costs.

There is a conflict between:

- the desire to minimise holding costs, by ordering in small quantities at frequent intervals; and

- the desire to minimise order costs, by placing large orders at infrequent intervals.

An inventory ordering and holding policy that minimises the total costs of holding inventory and ordering inventory combined (given a constant purchase price per unit of material regardless of order quantity) is to purchase materials in their **economic order quantity** (EOQ). The EOQ is the purchase order quantity that minimises total order costs plus inventory (stock) holding costs.

Running out of inventory (known as a **stockout**) also incurs costs. Customers might go elsewhere if finished goods are not in inventory when they want to buy them. Similarly, production will be disrupted if raw materials inventory is not on hand when required due to a stockout. **Buffer inventory (or buffer stock) which is also known as safety inventory (or safety stock),** is a basic level of inventory held to cover unexpected demand or uncertainty of lead time for the item of inventory. A further problem for management could be to decide how much buffer inventory to hold for each inventory item, to minimise the combined costs of:

- stockouts if the buffer inventory is not held; and

- the additional inventory holding costs that arise from having buffer inventory.

Clearly it is important to think carefully about the right level of inventory to hold so as to minimise the total associated costs.

Three questions about inventory control have to be resolved:

- in what quantities to order an item of inventory
- when to re-order
- what system to use for monitoring inventory levels.

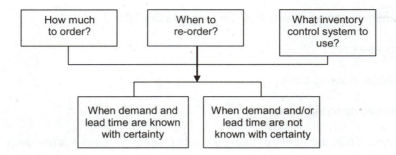

3 ECONOMIC ORDER QUANTITY (EOQ)

3.1 CALCULATING THE ECONOMIC ORDER QUANTITY

Ordering in large quantities reduces the annual costs of ordering. On the other hand, average inventory levels will be higher and so inventory holding costs increase. The economic order quantity, assuming there are no available bulk purchase discounts, is the quantity that minimises the combined costs of ordering and holding inventory.

Definition   **Economic order quantity** (EOQ) is the order quantity for an item of inventory that will minimise the combined costs of ordering and holding inventory over a given period of time, say each year.

The economic order quantity for an item of inventory is calculated on the basis of the following assumptions.

- There should be no stockout of the item.
- There is no buffer inventory (buffer stock).
- A new delivery of the inventory item is received from the supplier at the exact time that existing inventory runs out.
- The inventory item is used up at an even and predictable rate over time.
- The delivery lead time from the supplier is predictable and reliable.

There is a formula for calculating the economic order quantity for any item of inventory, given these assumptions, which is:

$$EOQ = \sqrt{\frac{2C_o D}{C_H}} \quad \text{where}$$

     C_o is the cost of placing an **order** of the inventory item

     C_H is the annual cost of **holding** one unit of the inventory

     D   is the annual **demand** for the inventory item

     Q   is the order **quantity**   *Economic Order Quantity*

MATERIAL INVENTORY CONTROL : CHAPTER 5

Note: Holding costs are often based on average inventory held which are estimated as $\frac{\text{Order quantity}}{2}$

[handwritten: Average Inventory one that travels throughout the year]

Total holding costs are therefore $\frac{EOQ}{2} \times$ Cost of holding one unit.

Example

Watton Ltd is a retailer of beer barrels. The company has an annual demand of 36,750 barrels. The barrels cost $12 each. Fresh supplies can be obtained immediately, but ordering costs and the cost of carriage inwards are $200 per order. The annual cost of holding one barrel in inventory is estimated to be $1.20.

$$EOQ = \sqrt{\frac{2C_oD}{C_H}}$$

For Watton, EOQ $= \sqrt{\frac{2 \times 200 \times 36{,}750}{1.20}}$

= 3,500 barrels

Total annual costs = Holding costs + Re-ordering costs

[handwritten: (Average Inventory × Cost of Holding) + (No of Orders × Cost of Placing 1 Order)]

= (Average inventory) × (C_H) + Number of re-orders pa × C_o

[handwritten: EOQ × C_H / D / Cost per order]

$= \frac{3{,}500 \times \$1.20}{2} + \frac{36{,}750 \times \$200}{3{,}500}$

= $2,100 + $2,100

= $4,200

ACTIVITY 1

Demand for a company's product is about 600,000 units per annum. It costs $3 to keep one unit in inventory for one year. Each time an order is placed, administrative costs of $40 are incurred.

How many units should the company order at a time so as to minimise the costs of ordering and holding inventory?

For a suggested answer, see the 'Answers' section at the end of the book.

[handwritten: Cost of Product will only be used to Calculate → Holding Cost]

MA 2 : MANAGING COSTS AND FINANCES

3.2 EOQ AND BULK PURCHASE DISCOUNTS

Frequently, discounts are offered for large quantity orders. These are often called bulk purchase discounts. The problem to consider is that if the order quantity to obtain the bulk discount is larger than the EOQ, i.e. is the discount worth taking?

To minimise costs, it is necessary to identify the order quantity that minimises the total costs of holding inventory plus ordering inventory plus the material purchase costs.

The problem may be solved by the following procedure.

1. Calculate the EOQ, ignoring discounts.

2. If the EOQ is smaller than the minimum purchase quantity to obtain a bulk discount, calculate the total for the EOQ of the annual inventory holding costs, inventory ordering costs and inventory purchase costs.

3. Recalculate the annual inventory holding costs, inventory ordering costs and inventory purchase costs for a purchase order size that is only **just large enough** to qualify for the bulk discount.

4. Compare the total costs when the order quantity is the EOQ with the total costs when the order quantity is just large enough to obtain the discount. Select the minimum cost alternative.

5. If there is a further discount available for an even larger order size, repeat the same calculations for the higher discount level.

Example

In the earlier example of Watton, suppose additionally that a 2% discount is available on orders of at least 5,000 barrels and that a 2.5% discount is available if the order quantity is 7,500 barrels or above. Given this information, would the least-cost order quantity still be 3,500 barrels?

Annual costs:

Av Holding Cost

	$
Order quantity = EOQ of 3,500 barrels	
Purchase costs (36,750 × $12) Av	441,000
Annual holding costs (see earlier) 1750 × 1.20	2,100
Annual ordering costs (see earlier) 10.5 × 200	2,100
Total costs	445,200

	$
Order quantity = 5,000 barrels	
Purchase costs (36,750 × $12 × 98%)	432,180
Annual holding costs ($1.20 × 5,000/2)	3,000
Annual ordering costs ($200 × 36,750/5,000)	1,470
Total costs	436,650

Order quantity = 7,500 barrels

	$
Purchase costs (36,750 × $12 × 97.5%)	429,975
Annual holding costs ($1.20 × 7,500/2)	4,500
Annual ordering costs ($200 × 36,750/7,500)	980
Total costs	435,455

Total costs are minimised with an order size of 7,500 barrels.

Note:

When annual inventory holding cost is an interest cost (given as a percentage of the purchase cost), if inventory is bought on a bulk purchase discount, the cost of holding one unit of inventory for one year will be reduced accordingly. Suppose that in the example above the cost of holding barrels is 10% of the purchase cost each year. By purchasing in order quantities of 7,500 and obtaining a discount of 2.5%, the annual cost of holding one barrel in inventory is not $1.20 (10% of $12) but $1.17 (10% of 97.5% of $12).

4 INVENTORY RE-ORDER LEVEL

The second problem in inventory control concerns the point at which a new order should be placed with a supplier.

The re-order level is the level of inventory at which a fresh order is placed with a supplier.

The lead time is the time gap that arises between an order being placed and its eventual delivery. If the demand and lead time are known with certainty then an exact re-order level may be calculated.

ACTIVITY 2

Return to the original Watton example. Assume that the company adopts the EOQ of 3,500 barrels as its order quantity and that it now takes two weeks for an order to be delivered.

Required:

(a) How frequently will the company place an order?

(b) How much inventory will it have on hand when the order is placed?

For a suggested answer, see the 'Answers' section at the end of the book.

In the real world, however, both the supply lead time and the demand for the inventory item during the lead time will vary. To avoid a stockout, the order must be placed so as to leave some buffer inventory (safety stock) if demand and lead time follow the average pattern. The problem is again to decide how to minimise the combined costs of holding higher levels of buffer inventory and the stockout costs if the buffer inventory is low.

You only need to be aware of this problem in general terms, however. For the purpose of your examination, it will be assumed that buffer inventory will be kept at a high enough level to reduce the risk of a stockout to zero. This means that the re-order level must be high enough to cover any foreseeable level of demand for the item of inventory during the lead time period between placing an order and its eventual delivery.

MA 2 : MANAGING COSTS AND FINANCES

4.1 RE-ORDER LEVEL TO AVOID STOCKOUTS, WITH UNCERTAIN DEMAND AND LEAD TIME

When the demand for an item of inventory is uncertain, because it varies from day to day or week to week, and when the supply lead time is variable, the re-order level that avoids any risk of a stockout during the lead time is:

Re-order level = Maximum supply lead time (in days or weeks) × Maximum daily or weekly demand for the item.

Example

A company operates a fixed re-order level of inventory control, and sets the re-order level so as to avoid the risk of stockouts. It is trying to establish the re-order level for a new inventory item, JK6. The daily demand for JK6 is expected to be not less than 60 tonnes and not more than 100 tonnes. The lead time between placing an order and receiving delivery from the supplier will be between one and three days.

What should be the re-order level for JK6?

Solution

Re-order level = 100 tonnes × 3 days = 300 tonnes.

If it is company policy to hold a required level of safety stock (buffer inventory) then the re-order level is calculated in a slightly different way.

Re-order level = Safety stock + (supply lead time × demand)

Example

A company is trying to establish the re-order level for a new item of inventory, Product X. The daily demand for this product is 50 units and the lead time between placing an order and receiving delivery from the supplier is 4 days. It is company policy to hold a safety stock level of 10 units.

Solution *[Buffer]*

Re-order level = Safety stock + (supply lead time × demand)

$\qquad$ = 10 + (50 × 4)

$\qquad$ = 10 + 200

$\qquad$ = 210 units

4.2 CONTROL LEVELS OF INVENTORY

When the so-called fixed re-order level system is used, it is usual to identify two other control levels for each inventory item, in addition to the re-order level. These are the minimum and maximum stock control levels (inventory control levels) for the item.

If the quantity held of an inventory item goes below the minimum control level, or above the maximum control level, a control message should be given to the manager responsible for inventory, for example the stores manager. The message should alert the manager to the fact that the inventory item and its inventory levels should be monitored carefully, and where necessary control measures should be taken. For example, if an item of inventory falls below its minimum control level, action might be taken to check with the supplier when the next delivery of the inventory should be received.

4.3 MINIMUM INVENTORY CONTROL LEVEL

The minimum stock (inventory) control level for an item of inventory is a warning level. If inventory falls to its minimum control level, management should check that a new delivery of the item will be received from the supplier before stockout occurs. Emergency action to replenish might be required.

The **minimum inventory control level** is calculated as:

Re-order level – Average expected demand for the inventory item during the average lead time

This can be stated as:

Re-order level – (Average demand for the item each day/month × Average length of lead time in days/months)

ACTIVITY 3

Calculate the minimum stock (inventory) control level from the following data:

Re-order level	3,600 units
Average lead time	5 days
Minimum usage	300 units per day
Maximum usage	500 units per day

For a suggested answer, see the 'Answers' section at the end of the book.

4.4 MAXIMUM INVENTORY CONTROL LEVEL

Another useful control level for inventory is the maximum stock (inventory) control level. This is the maximum quantity of an inventory item that should ever be held in store. If actual inventory levels exceed this quantity, something unusual must have happened. Either inventory must have been re-ordered before it reached the re-order level, the quantities consumed in the lead time must have been much lower than usual, or the lead time was shorter than expected.

The **maximum stock (inventory) control level** is the re-order quantity plus the re-order level minus the minimum quantity of inventory that should ever be consumed during the minimum lead time.

Expressed in a different way, the maximum stock (inventory) control level is therefore:

Re-order quantity plus Re-order level minus (Minimum demand per day/week × Minimum lead time in days/weeks)

Example

Z Limited places an order of 500 units, to replenish its inventory of a particular component whenever the inventory balance is reduced to 300 units. The order takes at least four days to be delivered and Z Limited uses at least 50 components each day. What is the maximum inventory control level?

Solution

The maximum inventory control level is: 500 + 300 − (50 × 4) = 600 units.

KAPLAN PUBLISHING

ACTIVITY 4

Calculate the re-order level, minimum stock (inventory) control level and maximum stock (inventory) control level from the following data.

Minimum lead time	4 days
Average lead time	5 days
Maximum lead time	7 days
Maximum usage	500 units per day
Minimum usage	300 units per day
Re-order quantity	5,400 units

For a suggested answer, see the 'Answers' section at the end of the book.

5 MATERIALS COSTING AND INVENTORY CONTROL

The previous chapter described the system for costing materials. This chapter has focused on inventory control systems.

The materials costing system is based on stores ledger records, and its purpose is to value inventory, and issues of materials from store. An inventory control system is concerned with monitoring inventory levels, keeping inventory losses to a minimum and minimising the costs of holding and ordering inventory (and avoiding or controlling the costs of any stockouts).

There is a relationship between these two systems, because inventory records need to be accurate. Accuracy is lost whenever errors or unrecorded inventory losses occur, and periodic comparisons of the stores ledger with the physical inventory held should be carried out through stocktakes.

CONCLUSION

Effective inventory control is important, particularly for many manufacturing businesses where raw material costs are high. Purchasing costs, holding costs, ordering costs and stockout costs must all be considered and minimised in total.

MATERIAL INVENTORY CONTROL : CHAPTER 5

KEY TERMS

Buffer stock – level of inventory held for emergencies.

Stockout – running out of inventory.

Stocktake – counting and recording physical quantities of inventory.

Lead time – the time between when an order is placed and the receipt of the inventory.

Economic Order Quantity – the order quantity that minimises ordering and holding costs.

Re-order level – Maximum lead time × Maximum demand.

Minimum inventory control level – Re-order level – (Average demand × Average lead time).

Maximum inventory control level – Re-order quantity + Re-order level – (Minimum demand × Minimum lead time).

Average stockholding – order quantity/2 = EOQ/2.

SELF TEST QUESTIONS

		Paragraph
1	What is a stockout?	2
2	What are the possible costs of a stockout?	2
3	What is buffer stock (inventory)?	2
4	Which combined costs are minimised when a inventory re-order quantity is the EOQ?	3.1
5	What is the formula for the inventory re-order level in a fixed re-order level system?	4.1
6	What is the formula for the minimum stock (inventory) control level in a fixed re-order level system?	4.3
7	What is the formula for the maximum stock (inventory) control level in a fixed re-order level system?	4.4

KAPLAN PUBLISHING

MA 2: MANAGING COSTS AND FINANCES

EXAM-STYLE QUESTIONS

The following information is to be used for questions 1 and 2.

A national chain of tyre fitters holds a popular tyre in inventory for which the following information is available:

Average usage	140 tyres per day
Minimum usage	90 tyres per day
Maximum usage	175 tyres per day
Lead time	10 to 16 days
Re-order quantity	3,000 tyres

1 Based on the data above, at what level of inventory should a replenishment order be issued?

    A   2,240

    B   2,800

    C   3,000

    D   5,740

2 Based on the data above, what is the maximum inventory control level?

    A   2,800

    B   3,000

    C   4,900

    D   5,800

The following information is to be used for questions 3 and 4.

A large retailer with multiple outlets maintains a central warehouse from which the outlets are supplied. The following information is available for Part Number SF525.

Average usage	350 per day
Minimum usage	180 per day
Maximum usage	420 per day
Lead time for replenishment	11 – 15 days
Re-order quantity	7,000 units
Re-order level	6,300 units

MATERIAL INVENTORY CONTROL : **CHAPTER 5**

3   Based on the data above, what is the maximum inventory control level?

   A   5,250

   B   6,500

   C   11,320

   D   12,800

4   What is the minimum stock (inventory) control level?

   A   200

   B   1,750

   C   2,450

   D   4,520

5   The following are all examples of stockout costs except:

   A   Loss of revenue from customers

   B   Loss of bulk purchase discount

   C   Idle time payments to workers

   D   Premium paid to supplier for urgent order.

6   A manufacturing organisation uses 5,000 kg of a raw material evenly over a period. The purchase price is $6.50 per kg and the holding cost per period is 10% of purchase price. If the order quantity is 500 kg and a buffer inventory of 100 kg is held, the total holding cost of the raw material in the period is:

   A $195

   B $227.50

   C $325

   D $3,250

The following information is relevant to questions 7 and 8

The following data relates to an item of raw material:

Cost of the raw material	$10 per unit
Usage per day	100 units
Minimum lead time	20 days
Maximum lead time	30 days
Cost of ordering material	$400 per order
Inventory holding cost	10% pa
Working days per annum	240

KAPLAN PUBLISHING   87

MA 2 : MANAGING COSTS AND FINANCES

7   The reorder level is:

    A   2,000 units

    B   2,400 units

    C   2,500 units

    D   3,000 units

8   The reorder quantity is:

    A   3,000 units

    B   4,000 units

    C   4,382 units

    D   4,644 units

For the answers to these questions, see the 'Answers' section at the end of the book.

Chapter 6

ACCOUNTING FOR LABOUR

NB — Direct v Indirect, Bonuses, Efficiency Ratio

In this chapter we look at the cost of labour. We begin by looking at the ways in which employees are paid, and the elements of pay in the payroll. We shall then go on to explain the distinctions between direct and indirect labour costs. The procedures for accounting for labour costs will then be described, and finally certain aspects of labour cost control will be explained, such as monitoring labour turnover and productivity. This chapter covers syllabus area B2.

CONTENTS

1. Labour remuneration
2. Accounting for payroll
3. Relationship between payroll accounting and labour costing
4. Direct and indirect labour costs
5. Documentation of labour time
6. Labour turnover
7. Labour efficiency and utilisation

LEARNING OUTCOMES

At the end of this chapter you should be able to:

- explain, illustrate and evaluate labour remuneration methods
- describe the operation of a payroll accounting system
- distinguish between direct and indirect labour costs
- describe the procedures and documentation required to ensure the correct coding, analysis and recording of direct and indirect labour
- describe and illustrate the accounting for labour costs
- discuss the relationship between the labour costing system and the payroll accounting system
- explain the causes and costs of, and calculate, labour turnover
- describe and illustrate measures of labour efficiency and utilisation (efficiency, capacity utilisation, production volume and idle time ratios).

1 LABOUR REMUNERATION

Most employees are paid a basic wage or salary. They might also earn additional payments, in the form of a bonus or for working overtime. Some employees do not earn a basic wage, but instead are paid according to the amount of output they produce (i.e. they are paid a 'piecework' rate).

You need to understand these basic elements of remuneration, so that you can calculate the cost of labour in an organisation.

1.1 FIXED BASIC SALARIES OR WAGES

A salary is a fixed basic amount of pay, usually payable every month. The amount of the basic salary is fixed for a given period of time.

The cost might be expressed as an annual salary such as $24,000 per year or as a weekly rate such as $461.50 per week.

Employees who are paid a fixed basic salary or wage are required to work a minimum number of hours, and in many organisations, they are not paid extra if they work for longer than this minimum. However, in other organisations, employees who work longer than the minimum number of hours each week or month are entitled to overtime payments.

1.2 PAYMENT FOR EACH HOUR WORKED

Time-rate employees are paid for the actual number of hours of attendance in a period, usually each week. A rate of pay will be set for each hour of attendance.

For employees who are paid for the hours they work, it is obviously extremely important to keep accurate records of the actual number of hours of attendance for each employee.

Example

An employee is paid $5.50 per hour and is expected to work at least a 48-hour week. What would he be paid for a standard 48-hour week?

Solution

48 hours × $5.50 = $264.00

ACTIVITY 1

An employee is paid $5.86 per hour and works 31.5 hours in a particular week. What would be the employee's wage for that week?

For a suggested answer, see the 'Answers' section at the end of the book.

1.3 PIECEWORK

Piecework is also known as payment by results or output-related pay. It is an alternative to time-related pay and fixed basic pay.

Definition   **Piecework** is where a fixed amount is paid per unit of output achieved irrespective of the time spent.

Example

If the amount paid to an employee is $3 per unit produced and that employee produces 80 units in a week how much should be paid in wages?

Solution

80 units × $3 = $240

As far as an employee is concerned piecework or payment by results means that he can earn whatever he wishes within certain parameters. The harder that he works and the more units that he produces then the higher will be his earnings.

From the employer's point of view, the employees are paid for what they produce, not the hours they work. This can help to control costs.

Piecework is not common in the UK for full-time workers, simply because it is not popular with employees. Piecework rates are often low, and it is difficult to earn a reasonable amount of pay without working long hours. In addition, the employee gets no income during holidays or when he or she is unable to work through illness.

There are two other problems associated with payment by results. One is the problem of accurate recording of the actual output produced. The amount claimed to be produced determines the amount of pay and, therefore, is potentially open to abuse unless it can be adequately supervised.

The second problem is that of the maintenance of the quality of the work. If the employee is paid by the amount that is produced then the temptation might be to produce more units but of a lower quality.

Conclusion   Basic payment methods for employees will either be time-related or output-related. Time-related methods are either a fixed basic salary or wage for a minimum number of hours per month or week, or a rate per hour worked. Output-related methods of payment are some sort of piecework payment.

1.4 VARIATIONS OF PIECEWORK

Basic piece-rate payments are a set amount for each unit produced e.g. $2.60 per unit. However, such systems are rare in practice and there are two main variations that could be viewed in a similar way to a bonus.

A **piece-rate with guarantee** operates to give the employee some security if the employer does not provide enough work in a particular period. The way that the system works is that if an employee's earnings for the amount of units produced in the period are lower than the guaranteed amount, then the guaranteed amount is paid instead.

MA 2 : MANAGING COSTS AND FINANCES

Example

Jones is paid $3.00 for every unit that he produces but he has a guaranteed wage of $28.00 per eight-hour day. In a particular week he produces the following number of units:

Monday	12 units
Tuesday	14 units
Wednesday	9 units
Thursday	14 units
Friday	8 units

Calculate Jones's wage for this week.

Solution

Total weekly wage

	$
Monday (12 × $3)	36
Tuesday (14 × $3)	42
Wednesday (guarantee)	28
Thursday (14 × $3)	42
Friday (guarantee)	28
	176

ACTIVITY 2

Continuing with the example of Jones above, what would be his weekly wage if the guarantee were for $140 per week rather than $28 per day?

For a suggested answer, see the 'Answers' section at the end of the book.

A **differential piecework system** is where the piece-rate increases as successive targets for a period are achieved and exceeded.

This will tend to encourage higher levels of production and acts as a form of bonus for payment by results for employees who produce more units than the standard level.

ACTIVITY 3

Payment by results rates for an organisation are as follows:

Up to 99 units per week	$1.50 per unit
100 to 119 units per week	$1.75 per unit
120 or more units per week	$2.00 per unit

If an employee produces 102 units in a week how much will he be paid?

For a suggested answer, see the 'Answers' section at the end of the book.

KAPLAN PUBLISHING

ACCOUNTING FOR LABOUR : CHAPTER 6

1.5 OVERTIME

If an employee works more than the number of hours set by the organisation as the working week, the additional hours worked are known as overtime. In many organisations employees who work overtime are paid an additional amount per hour for those extra hours that they work.

When the rate per hour for overtime is higher than the basic rate of pay in normal working hours, the additional pay per hour is known as **overtime premium**. For example, suppose that employees are paid a basic rate of $6 per hour, with overtime paid at time and a half, or at 50% above the basic rate, the overtime premium would be $3 per hour.

Example

The basic hourly rate of an employee is $7.20. Any overtime is paid at 125% of his normal hourly rate.

What is the amount paid for each hour of overtime, and what is the overtime premium?

Solution

Rate per hour in overtime = $7.20 × 125% = $9.00.

The overtime premium is $7.20 × 25% = $1.80.

In costing, it is important to distinguish, between the basic rate of pay and the overtime premium. This is because it is usual to treat overtime premium as an indirect labour cost, even when the basic rate of pay is a direct labour cost.

The overtime rate is only paid for the hours worked over the basic hours. The basic hours are paid at the basic rate.

ACTIVITY 4

An employee's basic week is 40 hours at a rate of pay of $5 per hour. Overtime is paid at 'time and a half'.

What is the wage cost of this employee if he works for 45 hours in a week?

For a suggested answer, see the 'Answers' section at the end of the book.

Overtime and fixed pay employees

If an employee's pay is a fixed weekly, monthly or annual amount rather than an hourly rate of pay, then any overtime payment will still normally be expressed in terms of a percentage of the basic hourly rate. It is, therefore, necessary to convert the salary into an effective hourly rate based on the standard working week of the organisation.

MA 2 : MANAGING COSTS AND FINANCES

ACTIVITY 5

An employee is paid an annual salary of $19,500. The standard working week for the organisation is 38 hours per week and the employee is paid for 52 weeks of the year. Any overtime that this employee works is paid at time and a half.

What is the hourly rate for this employee's overtime?

For a suggested answer, see the 'Answers' section at the end of the book.

1.6 BONUSES

Bonuses are payments to employees on top of their basic pay and any overtime payments. They may be paid to employees for a variety of reasons. An individual employee, a department, a division or indeed the entire organisation may have performed particularly well and it is felt by the management that a bonus is due to some or all of the employees.

The basic principle of a bonus payment is that the employee is rewarded for any additional income or savings in cost to the organisation. This may be for example because the employee has managed to save a certain amount of time on the production of a product or a number of products. This time saving will save the organisation money and the amount saved will tend to be split between the organisation and the employee on some agreed basis.

There are many different types of bonus arrangements. However, these different arrangements can be categorised as:

- a collective bonus scheme for all employees. In general a bonus will be paid to employees if the organisation as a whole has performed well in the latest period. Some of the profits from this above average performance will be shared with the employees in the form of a bonus. This is known as a profit-sharing bonus

- a collective bonus scheme for a limited group of employees. In some organisations bonuses may be determined on a departmental or divisional basis. If a particular department or division performs well then the employees in that department or division will receive some sort of bonus

- individual bonus schemes for employees.

Definition A **flat rate bonus** is where all employees are paid the same amount of bonus each regardless of their individual salary.

The principle behind such a payment is that all of the employees have contributed the same amount to earning the bonus no matter what their position in the organisation or their salary level.

Example

Suppose that a small business made a profit of $100,000 in the previous quarter and the managing director decided to pay out $20,000 of this as a flat rate bonus to each employee. The business has 50 employees in total including the managing director earning a salary of $48,000 per annum and Chris Roberts, his secretary, who earns $18,000 per annum.

How much would the managing director and Chris Roberts each receive as bonus for the quarter?

Solution

Total bonus	$20,000
Split between 50 employees ($20,000/50) =	$400 per employee
Managing director's bonus	$400
Chris Roberts's bonus	$400

A **percentage bonus scheme** is an alternative scheme to a flat rate bonus scheme.

Definition A **percentage bonus** is where the amount paid to each employee as bonus is a set percentage of that employee's annual salary.

The principle behind this method of calculating the bonus payable is to give a larger bonus to those with higher salaries in recognition that they have contributed more to the earning of the bonus than those with a lower salary.

In the above example, if the bonus payable were 1.5% of annual salary, the managing director would receive $720 and Chris Roberts would receive $270.

Productivity-related bonuses

A productivity-related bonus is a bonus whereby an employee (or group of employees) are paid extra for completing their work in less than the expected amount of time. In other words, if employees achieve higher-than-expected productivity, they are rewarded.

The principle of a productivity-related bonus or incentive scheme is to encourage the employees affected to achieve additional output in the time they work.

The basis of bonus schemes in these instances is to set a predetermined standard time (or target time) for the performance of a job or production of a given amount of output. If the job is completed in less than the standard time or more than the given output is achieved in the standard time then this will mean additional profit to the employer.

This additional profit will then be split between the employer and the employee in some agreed manner.

Example

It is expected that it will take 90 minutes for an employee to make a product. If the employee makes the product in 60 minutes what is the saving to the employer if the employee's wage rate is $5.00 per hour?

Solution

Time saving = 30 minutes

At a wage rate of $5.00 per hour the cost saving is $2.50.

In a productivity-related bonus scheme, the employee will be rewarded with a share of the cost saving. For example, if the employee receives half of the saving, the bonus would be paid at the rate of $2.50 per hour saved, which in the case of this example would amount to a bonus of $1.25.

Conclusion This employee's efficient work has saved the organisation $2.50. The basis of a bonus scheme for time-rate workers is that a proportion of this $2.50 should be paid to the employee as a bonus. The size of the bonus is for the employer to decide.

ACTIVITY 6

Employee's wage rate	$5.00 per hour
Time allowed for job	40 minutes
Time taken for job	25 minutes

The company's policy is to calculate the bonus payable to the employee as 35% of the time saved on the job. What is the bonus on this basis?

For a suggested answer, see the 'Answers' section at the end of the book.

2 ACCOUNTING FOR PAYROLL

Accounting for payroll is a part of the financial accounting system within an organisation. The payroll is prepared every time that employees are paid, which is usually every week or month.

The payroll is a list of each individual employee within the organisation, identifying the employee by name and employment number, and the department or cost centre for which the employee works. For each employee, the payroll is used to calculate:

- the employee's gross pay
- the employer's benefits contribution for the employee.

Gross pay is the employee's total remuneration. The employer's benefits contributions are additional payments of tax the employer must make to the government for the employee. For the organisation, the total cost of labour is the sum of gross pay and employer's benefits contributions, plus any contributions the employer makes to an employees' pension fund.

The payroll is also used to calculate the deductions from each employee's gross pay, for:

- income tax
- the employee's benefits contributions
- any contributions by the employee to a pension scheme
- any other deductions, such as payments for trade union membership.

The gross pay minus all deductions is the employee's net pay, or 'take home' pay, which is the cash payment by the employer to the employee.

The payroll therefore itemises the total labour cost for each employee, the deductions from pay and the net pay. It also shows the total cost of labour and the total amount of deductions, for each department or cost centre and for the organisation as a whole.

3 RELATIONSHIP BETWEEN PAYROLL ACCOUNTING AND LABOUR COSTING

With payroll accounting, the aim is to establish:

- the total amount of wages and salaries payable, deductions from pay and net pay

- the total cost of wages and salaries, for charging as an expense to the income statement.

There are two key accounts for recording payroll costs in a financial accounting system:

- a wages and salaries payable account

- a wages and salaries control account.

Illustrative examples of how these accounts are used are shown below. The wages and salaries payable account is used for recording deductions from pay and net pay. The wages and salaries control account is used to establish the total cost of labour for charging to the income statement.

Wages and salaries payable account

	$		$
Bank (net pay)	67,000	Wages and salaries control	100,000
Income tax payable	23,000		
Employees' Nat Insurance	10,000		
	100,000		100,000

Wages and salaries control account

	$		$
Wages and salaries payable	100,000	Income statement	115,000
Employer's Nat Insurance	15,000		
	115,000		115,000

With a labour costing system, the total wages and salaries cost (in the above example, $115,000) is analysed to calculate the costs of cost units. The first stage of this analysis is to separate direct labour costs from indirect labour costs, and account for these accordingly.

In a cost accounting system, instead of charging the wages and salaries cost to the income statement, the costs are therefore charged to work-in-progress (direct labour) or production overhead, administration overhead or sales and distribution overhead for indirect labour costs.

MA 2 : MANAGING COSTS AND FINANCES

Example

A manufacturing business has total wages and salaries costs in June of $115,000. These total costs consist of:

- direct labour costs — $37,000
- indirect production labour — $25,000
- administration labour costs — $24,000
- sales and distribution labour costs — $29,000

These labour costs should be accounted for as follows:

Wages and salaries control account

	$		$
		Work-in-progress	37,000
		Production overhead	25,000
		Administration overhead	24,000
		Sales and distribution overhead	29,000
			115,000

Work-in-progress

	$		$
Wages (direct labour)	37,000		

Production overheads

	$		$
Wages and salaries (indirect production labour)	25,000		

Administration overheads

	$		$
Wages and salaries	24,000		

Sales and distribution overheads

	$		$
Wages and salaries	29,000		

ACCOUNTING FOR LABOUR : CHAPTER 6

4 DIRECT AND INDIRECT LABOUR COSTS

(handwritten note: Overtime Premium / Idle Time)

Employees can be classified as either direct labour or indirect labour. Direct labour means employees who are directly involved in producing goods or services for customers. Indirect labour means employees who are not directly involved in this work. Examples of indirect labour employees in a manufacturing business are:

- employees working in administration or selling and distribution

- employees in departments that support production, but are not directly involved in production, such as staff in production planning, repairs and maintenance and stores

- employees in departments where production work is carried out, but who are not themselves directly involved in production work. These include department supervisors.

In production, direct labour employees are employees in production departments who work directly on making the products or completing the jobs or contracts for customers.

The total wages and salary costs of employees can be traced to individual departments/cost centres. All the labour costs of employees outside direct production departments are indirect labour, and their costs are indirect labour costs.

An aim in cost accounting is to identify direct labour costs and indirect labour costs. These are not the same as the costs of direct labour and indirect labour employees.

- All the costs of indirect labour employees are indirect labour costs.

- However, not all the costs of direct labour employees are treated as direct labour costs. Some of these costs are treated as indirect costs.

Costs of direct labour employees that are usually treated as indirect costs are:

- the costs of idle time

- the costs of overtime premium

- costs of labour time not spent in production, such as the cost of time spent on training courses, and the cost of payments during time off work through illness.

4.1 IDLE TIME

Definition   **Idle time** or **down time** is time paid for that is non-productive.

Idle time occurs in most organisations. What is important is that the amount of idle time and the reasons for it are accurately assessed, reported to management for corrective action if necessary and treated correctly in terms of allocation of the cost to products.

The effect of idle time is that for a set number of hours of work, if there is idle time or non-productive time within that period, then less will be produced than expected.

KAPLAN PUBLISHING

Example

Suppose that a workforce of 10 employees is expected to work a 35-hour week each. In the production time available it is expected that 175 units will be produced i.e. each unit requires two hours of labour.

Now suppose that the employees only actually work for 320 of those hours although they will be paid for the full 350 hours.

How many units would be likely to be made in that week? How would the 30 hours that were paid for but not worked be described?

Solution

The anticipated number of units to be produced would be 160 rather than the expected amount of 175. However, the workforce would still be paid for the full 350 hours.

The 30 hours paid for but not worked are an example of idle time.

Recording idle time

The amount of hours that are paid for but are not used for production represent wasted hours for the organisation and warrant close control from management.

To assist control, time booking procedures i.e. timesheets, job cards etc, should permit an analysis of idle time by cause.

Idle time can be classified as avoidable (or controllable) and unavoidable (or uncontrollable). Making this classification is often a matter for discretionary judgement. For example, are the idle time effects of a power cut avoidable? In most situations the answer is probably not, but if a standby generator was available but not used then the idle time would be classified as avoidable.

Avoidable idle time

The main causes of avoidable idle time are:

(a) production disruption: this could be idle time due to machine breakdown, shortage of materials, inefficient scheduling, poor supervision of labour, etc

(b) policy decisions: examples of this might include run-down of inventory, changes in product specification, retraining schemes, etc.

Idle time as an indirect labour cost

The labour costs of idle time cannot be charged directly to any individual products (or other cost units). Instead, they are treated as an indirect cost and included in production overhead costs.

4.2 OVERTIME

When direct labour works overtime, the basic rate of pay is treated as a direct labour cost. The overtime premium is usually treated as an indirect cost, and included in production overheads, although the premium can sometimes be a direct labour cost.

- If the overtime is worked for a specific reason, for example at the specific request of a customer to get a job finished more quickly, the full cost of the overtime work, including the overtime premium, should be treated as a direct labour cost (e.g. as a direct cost of the job).

- In all other circumstances, the overtime premium should be treated as an indirect cost, with only the basic labour cost (i.e. the overtime hours at the basic rate of pay) treated as a direct cost.

Example

During a particular month the workers in a factory worked on production for 2,500 hours. Of these 200 hours were hours of overtime of which 50 hours were to cover lost production and 150 were spent on an urgent job at the request of a customer.

The basic wage rate was $6.00 per hour and overtime was paid at the rate of time and a third.

Calculate the total wage cost for the month and show the amount of direct and indirect labour cost.

Solution

	$
Total wage cost	
(2,300 hours × $6) + (200 hours × $8)	$15,400

This can be broken down as follows:

	$
Direct costs	
Basic cost of direct workers 2,500 × $6	15,000
Overtime premium for urgent job 150 × $2	300
Total	15,300
Indirect cost	
Overtime premium for lost production	100
Total	100

4.3 IDENTIFYING DIRECT AND INDIRECT LABOUR COSTS

Within a costing system, the task of identifying the costs of indirect labour employees is quite straightforward. The data in the payroll can be used to identify the cost centre where the employee works, and the full cost of the employee is recorded as an indirect cost of the cost centre.

The task of separating the total costs of direct labour into direct and indirect labour costs is more complicated, because of idle time, overtime premium and other non-productive time. In addition, in order to measure the costs of different products or jobs, it is necessary to establish how much time the employee has spent working on each product or job. To do this, there has to be a system for recording direct labour times, and allocating the time spent to individual products or jobs.

MA 2 : MANAGING COSTS AND FINANCES

5 DOCUMENTATION OF LABOUR TIME

The most common methods of recording how much time has been spent on particular activities, products or jobs are:

- timesheets
- job sheets
- cost cards.

5.1 TIMESHEETS

Definition A **timesheet** is a record of how a person's time at work has been spent.

The total hours that an employee has worked in a day or week are shown on the employee's clock card but a breakdown of how those hours were spent will be shown on the timesheet.

The employee fills out his or her own timesheet on a daily, weekly or monthly basis depending upon the policies of the organisation.

The employee will enter his name, clock number and department at the top of the timesheet together with details of the work he has been engaged on in the period and the hours spent on that work.

The purpose of a timesheet for salaried employees is simply to allocate their costs to departments or products. No calculations of the amounts payable to the employee are necessary as these are fixed by the employee's salary agreement.

Example

In the week commencing 28 March 20X4 Bernard Gill from the maintenance department spent his time as follows:

Monday 28 March	9.30 am – 12.30 pm	Machine X
	1.30 pm – 5.30 pm	Machine X
Tuesday 29 March	9.30 am – 11.00 am	Machine X
	11.00 am – 12.30 pm	Office computer
	1.30 pm – 7.30 pm	Office computer
Wednesday 30 March	Sick leave	
Thursday 31 March	9.30 am – 12.30 pm	Machine L
	1.30 pm – 5.30 pm	Machine L
Friday 1 April	Holiday	

The working day for this organisation is 7 hours per day and any overtime is paid to a salaried employee of Bernard's grade at $8.10 per hour.

Required:

Write up Bernard Gill's timesheet for the week commencing 28 March 20X4. His clock card number is 925734.

Solution

TIMESHEET						
Name: Bernard Gill				**Clock Number:** 925734		
Department: Maintenance							
Week commencing: 28 March 20X4						
Date	Job	Start	Finish	Hours	Overtime Hrs	$
28/3	Machine X	9.30	5.30	7.0		
29/3	Machine X	9.30	11.00	1.5		
	Office computer	11.00	7.30	7.5	2	
30/3	Sick leave	9.30	5.30	7.0		
31/3	Machine L	9.30	5.30	7.0		
1/4	Holiday	9.30	5.30	7.0		
Total hours				37.0	2	
Total overtime payment						16.20
Foreman's signature						

5.2 JOB SHEETS

Job sheets take on an even greater importance for employees who are paid on a results or time basis. In these situations the sheet is a record of the products produced and it is also used to calculate the payment due to the employee.

Example

Sheila Green is an employee in a garment factory with a clock number of 73645. She is a machinist and she is paid $3.20 for each dress she machines, $4.10 for a pair of trousers and $2.50 for a shirt.

In the week commencing 28 March 20X4 she produces 23 dresses, 14 pairs of trousers and 21 shirts. It took her 28 hours to do this work. Draft her job sheet for that week.

MA 2 : MANAGING COSTS AND FINANCES

Solution

JOB SHEET						
Name: Sheila Green					**Clock Number:** 73645	
Department: Factory							
Week commencing: 28 March 20X4							
Product	*Units*	*Code*	*Price*	*Bonus*		*Total*
Dresses	23	DRE	3.20	–		73.60
Trousers	14	TRO	4.10	–		57.40
Shirts	21	SHI	2.50	–		52.50
Gross wages						183.50
Total hours						28
Foreman's signature:							
Date:							

A column is included in the timesheet for any bonus that the employee might earn. There is no overtime column as a payment by results employee does not earn overtime.

5.3 COST CARDS: JOB COSTING

Definition A **job cost card** is a card that records the costs involved in a particular job.

Instead of a record being kept of the work done by each employee, a record can be kept of the work performed on each job by all direct labour employees. This must of course be reconciled to the total amount of work recorded by the employees on their timesheets or clock cards.

ACTIVITY 7

A cake icer works on a number of cakes in a day and each one is costed as a separate job. The rate of pay for cake icing is $5.30 per hour. On 28 March 20X4 the icer worked on the following cakes:

28/3JN   3 hours

28/3KA   5 hours

Prepare job cards for these two jobs showing the amount of labour worked by the cake icer.

For a suggested answer, see the 'Answers' section at the end of the book.

6 LABOUR TURNOVER

Labour costs should be kept under control. There are various reasons why labour costs might be higher or lower than expected. Three such reasons are:

- labour turnover is higher or lower than usual

- labour efficiency or productivity might be better or worse than usual

- idle time might be high or low. Idle time is money spent on labour costs when no work is done. The cost of idle time is therefore a wasted expense.

Definition   **Labour turnover** is a measure of the speed at which employees leave an organisation and are replaced.

Labour turnover is often calculated as:

$$\frac{\text{Average annual number of leavers who are replaced}}{\text{Average number of employees}} \times 100\%$$

Labour turnover can be monitored over time, to see whether the rate is rising, falling or fairly stable. An organisation might have an idea of what is an acceptable rate of labour turnover, and compare the actual rate against this benchmark.

ACTIVITY 8

On average a company employs 7,000 workers but during the last year 200 of these workers have resigned and have had to be replaced.

What is the labour turnover for the year?

For a suggested answer, see the 'Answers' section at the end of the book.

6.1 COSTS OF LABOUR TURNOVER

Whenever employees leave an organisation, the organisation incurs a cost. The cost of replacing employees ('replacement costs') who have left is not just the obvious costs of advertising the replacement or paying an employment agency, and the costs of time spent interviewing, choosing and taking on the new employee. There are also a number of other less obvious replacement costs such as:

- the costs of training a new employee

- the loss of efficiency whilst new employees are learning the job

- the effect on the morale of the existing workforce when labour turnover is high, leading to a loss of efficiency.

Costs may also be incurred to reduce labour turnover. These costs are known as 'preventative costs' and may include:

- improving employee remuneration or benefits
- improving the working environment
- training existing employees and offering career progression.

ACTIVITY 9

The cost of labour turnover can be classified as preventative or replacement. Give three examples of each cost.

For a suggested answer, see the 'Answers' section at the end of the book.

6.2 CAUSES OF LABOUR TURNOVER

The employee records should show as clearly as possible the reasons for each employee leaving. If a particular cause is recurrent this should be investigated. However, often employees leaving do not give the full story of why they are leaving, therefore, any statistics gathered from this source should be treated with caution.

In some cases, the loss of employees is unavoidable. For example, employees might retire or move to a different part of the country (or to a different country altogether).

Sometimes, employees leave to take up a job somewhere else that offers more pay, or represents a career move.

Another cause of turnover can be dissatisfaction with the job, unpleasant working conditions, or poor interpersonal relationships with a supervisor or colleagues.

Management should try to identify causes of avoidable labour turnover, and think about whether any measures should be taken to try to reduce the turnover rate.

Conclusion High labour turnover has a high cost to a business that is not necessarily always obvious. Labour turnover should be closely monitored and reduced if possible.

7 LABOUR EFFICIENCY AND UTILISATION

Two other reasons why a workforce might produce more or less output than expected are labour efficiency and labour utilisation.

7.1 EFFICIENT AND INEFFICIENT LABOUR

Definition The labour force of an organisation is described as **efficient** if it produces more than the standard amount of goods in a set period of time.

If the labour force is efficient then it is working faster than anticipated or producing more goods than anticipated in a set period of time.

ACCOUNTING FOR LABOUR : **CHAPTER 6**

This might be because the employees are of a higher grade than anticipated or are more experienced or motivated or simply better at their job than the average employee.

Alternatively, it might be due to a better grade of material being used that is easier to work with or an improved design specification that requires fewer labour hours.

Definition   The labour force of an organisation is described as **inefficient** if it produces less than the standard amount of goods in a set period of time.

If the labour force is working more slowly than anticipated or producing less units in a set period of time than anticipated then the employees will be said to be inefficient.

This inefficiency might be because of poor morale within the workforce, use of inexperienced or below par employees or workers having an 'off day'.

It could also be due to the use of cheaper or lower grade materials that require more work or a change in the design specification that requires more hours.

7.2 EFFICIENCY RATIO

Labour efficiency or productivity can be measured by means of an **efficiency ratio**. The efficiency ratio compares the time actually taken to do the work and the time that would have been expected to do the work. The expected time to do a piece of work, such as the expected time to make one unit of a product, can be measured in standard hours.

Definition   A **standard hour** is the output expected in one hour of production at normal efficiency.

For example, if 2,000 units of an item are produced and the standard time to produce one unit is 15 minutes, the output produced represents 500 standard hours of work.

Similarly, if a firm makes 200 units of Product X which should take 2 hours per unit, and 500 units of Product Y which should take 30 minutes per unit, the output produced represents 650 standard hours (400 hours for X and 250 hours for Y).

Definition   The **efficiency ratio** is a ratio, expressed as a percentage, that compares the standard hours of work produced with the actual hours worked. When the output is produced in exactly the time expected, the efficiency ratio is 100%. When output is produced in less than the expected time, the ratio is higher than 100%.

The efficiency ratio is calculated as follows:

$$\frac{\text{Actual output measured in standard hours}}{\text{Actual production hours}} \times 100\%$$

The efficiency ratio is often referred to as the **productivity ratio**.

7.3 CAPACITY RATIO: LABOUR UTILISATION

A capacity ratio can be used to measure the utilisation of labour. Labour utilisation refers to how much labour time is used, compared to how much available time was expected.

Definition The **capacity ratio** is expressed as a percentage and compares the actual number of hours actively worked with the budgeted labour hours for the period.

$$\text{Capacity ratio} = \frac{\text{Actual hours worked}}{\text{Budgeted hours}} \times 100\%$$

7.4 PRODUCTION/VOLUME RATIO OR ACTIVITY RATIO

Definition The **production/volume ratio** assesses how the overall production level compares to planned levels, and is the product of the efficiency ratio and the capacity ratio.

Over 100% indicates that overall production is above planned levels and below 100% indicates a shortfall compared to plans.

The production/volume ratio is calculated as:

$$\frac{\text{Actual output measured in standard hours}}{\text{Budgeted production hours}} \times 100\%$$

The three ratios calculated above can be summarised diagrammatically as follows:

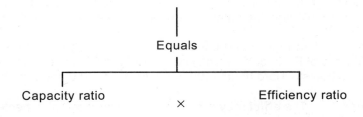

Conclusion Capacity ratio   –   a measure of utilisation

Efficiency ratio   –   a measure of productivity

Activity ratio   –   a measure of overall production

ACTIVITY 10

The budgeted output for a period is 2,000 units and the budgeted time for the production of these units is 200 hours.

The actual output in the period is 2,300 units and the actual time worked by the labour force is 180 hours.

Calculate the three ratios.

For a suggested answer, see the 'Answers' section at the end of the book.

NB Chapter

ACCOUNTING FOR LABOUR : CHAPTER 6

7.5 IDLE TIME RATIO

The idle time ratio is a another useful ratio because it gives an indication of the percentage of working hours that were lost as a result of the labour force being 'idle' during idle time.

Definition The **idle time ratio** shows the percentage of labour hours available that were lost because of idle time.

The idle time ratio is calculated as:

$$\frac{\text{Idle hours}}{\text{Total hours available}} \times 100\%$$

CONCLUSION

This chapter explained the different methods of remunerating employees and how payroll costs and labour costs are recorded. The distinction between direct and indirect labour costs has been explained.

Finally, ratios for monitoring and controlling labour turnover, efficiency and utilisation have been described.

We have now looked at two elements of cost, materials and labour. In the next chapter, we shall look at other expenses.

KEY TERMS

Overtime – time that is paid for, usually at a premium, over and above the basic hours for the period.

Overtime premium – the amount paid for overtime in excess of the basic rate of pay.

Piecework – where a fixed amount is paid per unit of output achieved irrespective of the time spent.

Flat rate bonus – where all employees are paid the same amount of bonus each regardless of their individual salary.

Percentage bonus – where the amount paid to each employee as bonus is a set percentage of that employee's annual salary.

Individual bonus schemes – those that benefit individual workers according to their own results.

Group bonus scheme – where the bonus is based upon the output of the workforce as a whole or a particular group of the workforce. The bonus is then shared between the individual members of the group on some pre-agreed basis.

Timesheet – a record of how a person's time at work has been spent.

Job card – a card that records the costs involved in a particular job.

Idle time or down time – time paid for that is non-productive.

KAPLAN PUBLISHING

MA 2 : MANAGING COSTS AND FINANCES

Direct labour cost – the cost of labour that is directly attributable to a cost unit. It consists of the cost of direct labour spent actively working on production, but usually excludes any overtime premium payments.

Indirect labour cost – labour overheads, consisting of all the labour costs of indirect workers plus the indirect labour costs of direct workers.

Labour turnover – the rate at which employees leave the organisation. A labour turnover ratio is measured as the numbers leaving in a period as a percentage of the average total number of employees in the period.

Efficiency ratio – comparison of the expected time for producing output compared with the actual time, expressed as a percentage.

Capacity ratio – comparison of the actual time worked with the budgeted time for the period, expressed as a percentage.

Production/volume ratio – assesses how the overall production level compares to planned levels, and is the product of the efficiency ratio and the capacity ratio.

Idle time ratio – this ratio shows the percentage of working hours available that were lost because of idle time.

SELF TEST QUESTIONS

		Paragraph
1	What is piecework?	1.3
2	What types of bonus scheme are there?	1.6
3	What are timesheets and how are they used?	5.1
4	What are job cost cards?	5.3
5	What is the formula for the labour turnover rate?	6
6	What is the formula for the labour efficiency ratio?	7.2

EXAM-STYLE QUESTIONS

1   A manufacturing firm is very busy and overtime is being worked.

   The amount of overtime premium contained in direct wages would normally be classed as:

   A   part of prime cost

   B   factory overheads

   C   direct labour costs

   D   administrative overheads

ACCOUNTING FOR LABOUR : CHAPTER 6

2 A contract cleaning firm estimates that it will take 2,520 actual cleaning hours to clean an office block. Unavoidable interruptions and lost time are estimated to take 10% of the operatives' time. If the wage rate is $4 per hour, what is the budgeted labour cost?

   A $10,080

   B $11,088

   C $11,200

   D $12,197

3 Which of the following would be classed as indirect labour?

   A   Assembly workers in a company manufacturing televisions

   B   A stores assistant in a factory store

   C   Plasterers in a construction company

   D   An audit clerk in a firm of auditors

4 Gross wages incurred in Department 1 in June were $135,000. The wages analysis shows the following summary breakdown of the gross pay:

	Paid to direct labour $	Paid to indirect labour $
Ordinary time	62,965	29,750
Overtime		
Basic pay	13,600	8,750
Premium	3,400	2,190
Shift allowance	6,750	3,495
Sick pay	3,450	650
	$90,165	$44,835

What is the direct wages cost for Department 1 in June?

   A $62,965

   B $76,565

   C $86,715

   D $90,165

For the answers to these questions, see the 'Answers' section at the end of the book.

Chapter 7

ACCOUNTING FOR OTHER EXPENSES

In this chapter we look at the costs of other expenses, apart from materials costs and labour costs. Other expenses include sub-contractors and other invoiced costs. Depreciation charges are also classified as expenses and we cover the main methods of calculating depreciation. This chapter covers syllabus area B3.

CONTENTS

1. Types of expense by function
2. Direct and indirect expenses
3. Accounting for expenses and expenses costing
4. Documentation for expenses
5. Capital and revenue expenditure
6. Depreciation

LEARNING OUTCOMES

At the end of this chapter you should be able to:

- describe the nature of expenses by function

- describe the procedures and documentation required to ensure the correct authorisation, coding, analysis and recording of direct and indirect expenses

- describe and calculate capital and revenue expenditure and the relevant accounting treatment

- calculate and explain depreciation charges using straight-line, reducing balance and machine hour and product unit methods

- discuss the relationship between the expenses costing system and the expense accounting system.

1 TYPES OF EXPENSE BY FUNCTION

An organisation will incur many different types of expense, other than expenses relating to materials and labour costs. There may be expenses associated with the manufacturing process or the factory, the selling process, general administration or the day-to-day running of the business and the financing of the business.

1.1 MANUFACTURING EXPENSES

Examples of expenses incurred during the manufacturing process include:

- the cost of power necessary for the machinery to be running
- the lighting and heating costs of the factory
- factory rental cost
- payments to external organisations for repair work or factory security operations
- insurance of the machinery
- depreciation of machinery.

1.2 SELLING AND DISTRIBUTION EXPENSES

During the process of selling the goods to the customer the types of expense that might be incurred include:

- advertising costs
- packaging costs
- costs of delivering the goods to the customer: vehicle depreciation and repairs, freight charges
- warehouse rental for storage of goods.

1.3 ADMINISTRATION EXPENSES

The everyday running of the organisation will involve many different expenses including the following types of item:

- rent of office buildings
- insurance of office buildings
- telephone bills
- postage costs
- depreciation of office equipment
- auditor's fees.

1.4 FINANCE EXPENSES

The costs of financing an organisation might include the following:

- loan interest
- lease charges if any equipment or buildings are leased rather than purchased.

2 DIRECT AND INDIRECT EXPENSES

To a cost accountant there are three types of business expenditure. These are materials, labour and expenses.

Definition **Expenses** are all business costs that are not classified as materials or labour costs.

Definition A **direct expense** is an expense that can be identified in full with a specific cost unit.

Examples – direct expenses

Direct expenses that may be attributed to a particular product or cost unit might include the following:

- running costs of a machine used only for one product
- packaging costs for a product
- royalties payable per product
- subcontractors' fees attributable to a single product or job
- the cost of machinery or equipment hired for a particular job or contract.

It is often difficult to trace an entire expense to a single cost unit, which means that most expenses are treated as indirect costs, and charged to a cost centre as an overhead.

Definition An **indirect expense** is expenditure which cannot be identified with a specific cost unit.

Conclusion The majority of materials and labour costs will be direct costs as they can be specifically attributed to cost units. The majority of expenses, however, will tend to be indirect costs as they will be items of expenditure that relate to a number of different products or cost units.

3 ACCOUNTING FOR EXPENSES AND EXPENSES COSTING

In a financial accounting system, expenses are accounted for by:

- debiting an appropriate expense account; and
- crediting the bank account, payables account or provision for depreciation account.

At the end of an accounting period, the expense account is cleared by:

- crediting the expense account with the total expense for the period; and
- debiting the income statement.

MA 2 : MANAGING COSTS AND FINANCES

In a costing system, expenses are not debited directly to the income statement. Instead:

- direct expenses are debited to the work-in-progress account

- indirect expenses are debited to a production overhead, administration overhead or sales and distribution overhead account.

By debiting expenses to work-in-progress or an overhead account, we are able to build up the costs of activities.

Overhead accounts are therefore used to build up the costs of indirect materials, indirect labour and indirect expenses. The following example might help to illustrate this process.

Example

The following costs have been recorded in a period:

Total depreciation	$25,000
Of which production machinery	$15,000
Office equipment	$4,000
Delivery vehicles	$6,000
Factory rental	$16,000
Advertising expenses	$22,000
Subcontractors' costs	$10,000

Solution

The accounting entry for depreciation is to credit the depreciation account and debit the appropriate overhead account. The accounting entry for other expenses is to credit the appropriate expenses account (one aggregate account has been used here but it would be equally correct to use individual accounts for each expense) and debit WIP with direct expenses and the appropriate overhead account with indirect expenses.

Equipment depreciation account

	$		$
		Production overhead	15,000
		Administration overhead	4,000
		Sales and distribution overhead	6,000
			25,000

Expenses

	$		$
Cash or payables		Production overheads	16,000
(Factory rental)	16,000	Sales and distribution overheads	22,000
(Advertising expenses)	22,000		
(Sub-contractors costs)	10,000	Work-in-progress	10,000

ACCOUNTING FOR OTHER EXPENSES : CHAPTER 7

Work-in-progress

	$		$
Expenses	10,000		

Production overheads

	$		$
Equipment depreciation	15,000		
Expenses (Factory rental)	16,000		

Administration overheads

	$		$
Equipment depreciation	4,000		

Sales and distribution overheads

	$		$
Equipment depreciation	6,000		
Expenses (Advertising)	22,000		

4 DOCUMENTATION FOR EXPENSES

Most expenses are documented in the form of an **invoice** from a supplier. For example, businesses receive invoices from external contractors, for rent, telephone expenses and electricity charges.

After the invoice has been checked and approved, a copy is sent to the cost accounting department, where the expense is allocated to a cost centre/cost code. (Direct expenses are allocated directly to the cost unit.)

The documentation for **non-current (fixed) asset depreciation** is the **non-current (fixed) asset register**, i.e. a record of the organisation's non-current assets. Each non-current asset can be associated with a particular cost centre, and the depreciation charge can be allocated directly to that cost centre as an overhead expense.

5 CAPITAL AND REVENUE EXPENDITURE

When a business spends money on an item it must be classified as either capital expenditure or revenue expenditure. The importance of the distinction between these two types of expenditure is in their different accounting treatments.

5.1 CAPITAL EXPENDITURE

Definition **Capital expenditure** is expenditure by a business on non-current (fixed) assets.

Definition **Non-current (fixed) assets** are assets of the business that are for long term use in the business.

Therefore when a business buys items of machinery, cars, computers, office furniture or a building these are classified as capital expenditure.

The accounting treatment of capital expenditure is that the cost of the asset is included as a non-current (fixed) asset in the statement of financial position of the business rather than being part of the expenses of the business in the income statement.

The cost is written off over the expected useful life of the asset in the form of a periodic **depreciation charge**. Depreciation of non-current assets is an expense for costing purposes and is usually an indirect expense of the cost centre using the asset.

Although depreciation is an expense, it is important to recognise that it does not represent a cash expenditure. Cash is paid when the asset is originally purchased. Recognising depreciation as a non-cash item is important when cost information is presented to management for decision-making purposes (as will be explained in a later chapter).

5.2 REVENUE EXPENDITURE — *APPEARS IN INCOME STATEMENT*

Definition   **Revenue expenditure** is all expenditure other than capital expenditure and represents day-to-day or operating expenses.

Revenue expenditure will therefore include expenditure on materials, wages, power costs, lighting and heating bills, telephone bills, rent, to name but a few.

The accounting treatment of revenue expenditure is that it is treated as an expense in the income statement in the period in which the expense is incurred.

Conclusion   The importance of the distinction between capital and revenue expenditure is in its accounting treatment. The cost of non-current assets, capital expenditure, is taken straight to the statement of financial position of the business and written off over time in the form of depreciation charges. The cost of all other items of expenditure, revenue expenditure, is taken in full to the income statement as an expense for the period.

6 DEPRECIATION

6.1 THE NATURE OF DEPRECIATION

Definition   **Depreciation** is the measure of the wearing out, consumption or other reduction in the useful economic life of a non-current asset.

Depreciation is a way of reflecting that when an asset is owned and used in a business there will be a cost to the business of using this asset. This will not just be the cost of running and maintaining the asset but also a cost in terms of using up some of the working life of the asset.

Depreciation is a method of charging some of the initial cost of a non-current asset to the accounts in each period that the asset is used. The reason for doing this is that the asset is being used to benefit the business by making goods or earning revenues, therefore a proportion of the asset's cost should be charged to the business as an expense in order to match with these revenues.

ACCOUNTING FOR OTHER EXPENSES : CHAPTER 7

Example

A machine is purchased at a cost of $10,000. It is expected to be used for five years in the business to make goods and will have no value at the end of that five year period. The machine will cost $60 each year to insure, $100 to maintain and service and approximately $150 of power to run it for a year.

What are the actual costs to the business associated with this machine, assuming that the annual charge for depreciation is the same amount each year?

Solution

Annual costs

	$
Insurance	60
Maintenance	100
Running costs	150
Depreciation ($10,000/5 years)	2,000

6.2 METHODS OF DEPRECIATION

Depreciation can conveniently be thought of as a method of spreading the cost of an asset (minus any expected residual value at the end of its useful life) over the years in which the asset is expected to be in use.

For example, suppose that a non-current asset costs $30,000 and has an expected useful life of 6 years and a residual value of $5,000 at the end of six years. The total amount of depreciation to charge will be $25,000 ($30,000 – $5,000) over six years. There are different ways in which this can be done. The methods you need to know are:

- straight-line method
- reducing balance method
- machine hours method
- product units method.

6.3 STRAIGHT-LINE METHOD

With the straight-line method of depreciation, the annual charge for depreciation is the same each year. It is calculated as:

$$\frac{\text{Cost less residual value}}{\text{Expected useful life (years)}}$$

When the residual value is zero, the total depreciation charge over the life of the asset will be the original cost of the asset. In such cases, the straight-line rate of depreciation can be expressed as a percentage of the original cost each year.

For example, if an asset has an expected useful life of five years and no residual value, the straight-line depreciation rate could be expressed as 20% of the asset cost.

KAPLAN PUBLISHING

ACTIVITY 1

Suppose that a vehicle is purchased for $48,000 and is expected to have a resale value of $20,250 in three years' time when the organisation disposes of it.

Calculate the annual depreciation charge for the car on a straight-line basis.

For a suggested answer, see the 'Answers' section at the end of the book.

6.4 REDUCING BALANCE METHOD

The net book value of a non-current asset is the amount at which the asset is stated in the statement of financial position. This is:

Cost	X
Less Accumulated depreciation charges to date	X
Equals Net book value	X

The reducing balance method of depreciation is where the percentage depreciation rate is applied to the net book value of the asset in order to calculate the annual depreciation charge.

As a result, the annual depreciation charge becomes smaller each year. It is at its largest in the first year and its smallest in the final year of use.

The reducing balance method is sometimes preferred to the straight-line method for assets such as motor vehicles that lose much of their market value soon after purchase.

Example

A lorry is purchased for $50,000 and is to be depreciated at a rate of 20% per annum using the reducing balance method. Calculate the depreciation charge for the first three years.

	$
Cost	50,000
Year 1 depreciation charge (20% × 50,000)	10,000
Net Book Value	40,000
Year 2 depreciation charge (20% × 40,000)	8,000
Net Book Value	32,000
Year 3 depreciation charge (20% × 32,000)	6,400
Net Book Value	25,600

ACTIVITY 2

Using the same information as before suppose that a vehicle is purchased for $48,000 and is expected to have a resale value of $20,250 in three years' time when the organisation will dispose of it.

Calculate the depreciation charge for each of the three years if a rate of 25% is applied, using the reducing balance method.

For a suggested answer, see the 'Answers' section at the end of the book.

6.5 MACHINE HOURS METHOD

The machine hours method of depreciation, as the name suggests, is sometimes used for non-current assets such as machinery, where it is considered appropriate to charge depreciation according to the use that has been made of the asset.

Depreciation is charged at a rate per hour for each hour that the asset is actually used in the period.

The rate of depreciation per hour is calculated as:

$$\frac{\text{Cost less residual value}}{\text{Expected total number of hours of use over the life of the asset}}$$

Since the machine hours method of calculating depreciation is based upon the actual usage of the asset rather than the passage of time, it is sometimes considered more appropriate for cost accounting purposes than other depreciation methods.

ACTIVITY 3

A machine has been purchased for $20,000 and has an estimated residual value of zero after the five years that it will be used by the organisation. During those five years it is estimated that the machine will be operational for 5,000 hours. In the first year of operations the machine was used for 1,800 hours.

Using the machine hours method of calculating depreciation what is the depreciation charge for the first year?

For a suggested answer, see the 'Answers' section at the end of the book.

6.6 PRODUCT UNITS METHOD

The product units method is expressed in the total number of units expected to be produced from an asset. It is typically used when assets have a production capacity over their life which is known. This is common in some machines (for example, a printing machine may only last for so many printed units).

The depreciation is computed in two steps:

1. Compute the "depreciation per unit" as follows:

$$\frac{\text{Cost less residual value}}{\text{Expected total number of units that can be produced over the life of the asset}}$$

2. Calculate is the actual depreciation expense, which is recorded on the income statement. Depreciation expense equals depreciation per unit multiplied by the number of units produced during the year.

Example

A machine costs $60,000 to buy and can produce a total of 12,000 units during its useful economic life, at the end of which it will be sold for $3,000. It is expected to produce 4,000 units this year. Calculate the depreciation charge for the year.

The depreciation per unit charge will be ($60,000 − $3,000) divided by 12,000 units = $4.75 per unit. So the charge for the year will be $4.75 x 4,000 units = $19,000.

CONCLUSION

Expenses can be a major cost for organisations which subcontract a high proportion of their work. The same principles apply to analysing and accounting for direct and indirect expenses as for labour and material costs. This enables the total direct costs of a cost unit and the total indirect cost of a cost centre to be identified. The method of attributing indirect costs to cost units to build up a full product cost will be considered in the next chapter.

KEY TERMS

Expenses – all business costs that are not classified as materials or labour costs.

Direct expense – an expense that can be identified in full with a specific cost unit.

Indirect expense – an expense that cannot be identified with a cost unit.

Capital expenditure – expenditure on non-current (fixed) assets.

Non-current (fixed) assets – the assets of the business that are for long term use in the business.

Revenue expenditure – day-to-day expenses or all expenditure other than capital expenditure.

Depreciation – a measure of the wearing out, consumption or other reduction in the useful economic life of a non-current asset.

ACCOUNTING FOR OTHER EXPENSES : CHAPTER 7

SELF TEST QUESTIONS

Paragraph

1 Give three examples of manufacturing expenses. 1.1

2 Define direct expenses. 2

3 Define indirect expenses. 2

4 In which cost ledger account are indirect production expenses recorded? 3

5 What is capital expenditure? 5.1

6 What is the accounting treatment of capital expenditure? 5.1

7 What is revenue expenditure? 5.2

8 Define depreciation. 6.1

9 How is the reducing balance method of depreciation applied? 6.4

10 How is the depreciation rate per hour calculated for the machine rate method of depreciation? 6.5

EXAM-STYLE QUESTIONS

1 All of the following costs relating to a machine in a manufacturing process would be classified as indirect expenses **except:**

    A   the cost of power to run the machine

    B   depreciation of the machine

    C   insurance of the machine

    D   lubricating oil for the machine

2 The accounting entry for the subcontractors' fees of freelance artists working on specialist pottery would be:

    A   Dr Work-in-progress   Cr Labour control account

    B   Dr Work-in-progress   Cr Expenses

    C   Dr Work-in-progress   Cr Production overhead control

    D   Dr Production overhead control   Cr Expenses

3   A machine has an estimated four-year life and a residual value of $2,500. It originally cost $20,000. The deprecation charge in Year 3, if the reducing balance method at 25% is used, is:

   A $2,812.50

   B $2,460.94

   C $4,375.00

   D $3,750.00

4   A new vehicle has an estimated six-year life and nil residual value. Depreciation is currently charged at 20% on a reducing balance method on this type of asset. The company is considering changing to a straight-line method of depreciation. Which of the following statements is correct?

   A   Depreciation would be higher in the first year if a straight-line method is used.

   B   The total depreciation charge over the whole life of the asset would be greater using the straight-line method.

   C   Depreciation would be lower in Year 1 if the straight-line method is used but higher in Year 6, compared to the existing method.

   D   Depreciation would be lower each year if the straight-line method is used

For the answers to these questions, see the 'Answers' section at the end of the book.

Chapter 8

ABSORPTION COSTING

In previous chapters, we have seen how costs can be classified as direct material costs, direct labour costs and overhead costs. This chapter explains how the costs of products or services are established using a system of costing known as absorption costing. In absorption costing, the main problem is how to charge a fair share of overhead costs to products or services. This chapter covers syllabus areas C1 and C2(c).

CONTENTS

1. Product costs and service costs
2. Treatment of overheads in absorption costing
3. Overhead allocation
4. Apportionment of overhead costs
5. Overhead analysis sheet
6. Service cost centre re-apportionment
7. The arbitrary nature of overhead apportionments
8. Overhead absorption
9. Under- and over-absorption of overheads
10. Accounting for production overheads
11. Investigating the causes of under- or over-absorbed overhead
12. Non-production overheads
13. Fixed, variable and semi-fixed overheads

MA 2 : MANAGING COSTS AND FINANCES

LEARNING OUTCOMES

At the end of this chapter you should be able to:

- explain the rationale for absorption costing

- describe the nature of production and service cost centres and their significance for production overhead allocation, apportionment and absorption

- describe the process of allocating, apportioning and absorbing production overheads to establish product costs

- apportion overheads to cost centres using appropriate bases

- re-apportion service cost centre overheads to production cost centres using direct and step down methods

- justify, calculate and apply production cost centre overhead absorption rates using labour hour and machine hour methods

- explain the relative merits of actual and pre-determined absorption rates

- describe and illustrate the accounting for production overhead costs, including the analysis and interpretation of over/under absorption

- describe and apply methods of attributing non-production overheads to cost units

- calculate product costs using the absorption costing method

- prepare profit statements using the absorption costing method.

1 PRODUCT COSTS AND SERVICE COSTS

Commercial organisations either sell products or provide services. They need to know what their products or services cost. There are several reasons for wanting to know about product costs and service costs.

- We need to know about costs in order to decide whether the products or services are profitable.

- In some cases, products or services might be priced by adding a profit mark-up on cost.

- In the case of products, closing inventory must be valued at its cost.

We have seen that the costs incurred by an organisation can be categorised as direct or indirect. Unlike direct costs, indirect costs cannot be associated directly with products or services.

Definition **Overheads** is a term for indirect costs.

A key issue with product costing and service costing is deciding what to do about overhead costs.

ABSORPTION COSTING : CHAPTER 8

Example

A company makes two products, X and Y. During a given period, the company makes 1,000 units of each product. The direct costs of Product X are $50,000 and the direct costs of Product Y are $80,000. Overhead costs for the period are $150,000.

If we want to establish a cost for Product X and Product Y, the direct costs of each product are easily established. But what about the overheads? Should each product be given a share of the overhead costs? If the overhead costs are to be divided between the two products, on what basis should the total cost be shared?

Definition **Absorption costing** is a method of costing in which the costs of an item (product or service or activity) are built up as the sum of direct costs and a fair share of overhead costs, to obtain a full cost or a fully-absorbed cost.

1.1 PRODUCT COSTS AND ABSORPTION COSTING

When costs are incurred, they can be recorded as:

- direct materials
- direct labour
- (sometimes) direct expenses; or
- overheads.

Overhead costs are charged to a cost centre (or 'responsibility centre'), which might represent:

- production overheads
- administration overheads
- selling and distribution overheads
- general overheads. However, general overheads are shared out between production, administration and selling and distribution overheads.

Fully-absorbed product costs can therefore be built up as follows (with illustrative figures included):

	$
Direct materials	12
Direct labour	8
Direct expenses	2
Total direct costs	22
Production overhead	16
Full production cost	38
Administration overhead	6
Selling and distribution overhead	10
Full cost of sale	54

KAPLAN PUBLISHING

127

MA 2 : MANAGING COSTS AND FINANCES

Notes:

1   In the statement of financial position, closing inventory is valued at its full production cost.

   This is consistent with the requirements for financial accounting. In any financial statements that are produced for external users (such as shareholders or the tax authorities), absorption costing must be used. In management accounts, which are only used internally by the business managers, the business can choose any method of stock valuation it wishes.

2   Absorption costing problems are concerned with building up the full production cost and therefore concentrate on production overheads. Non-production overheads may be charged as a period cost against profits or may be added to full production cost using a given percentage.

1.2 SERVICE COSTS AND ABSORPTION COSTING

Fully-absorbed service costs can be built up in the same way. A service business must first of all decide what a unit of service should be. For example:

- for a telecommunications business, a unit of service might be a cost per telephone call per minute or the cost of a communications link

- for a private hospital, a cost might be a cost per patient day

- for an electricity supply business, a unit cost might be a cost per unit of electricity supplied.

Service costs might be established as follows:

	$
Direct materials	2
Direct labour	10
Direct expenses	4
Total direct costs	16
Operating overhead	28
Full operating cost	44
Administration overhead	10
Selling and distribution overhead	16
Full cost of sale	70

1.3 FIXED AND VARIABLE OVERHEADS

Overhead costs might be fixed costs or variable costs. In absorption costing, production overheads, administration overheads and selling and distribution overheads might therefore be separated into their fixed and variable cost components.

In absorption costing for products, the full production cost of a product might therefore consist of direct materials, direct labour, direct expenses, variable production overhead and fixed production overhead.

- **Fixed overheads** remain the same whatever the level of output or activity during a period. It does not vary with changes in output levels or activity, but remains constant.

- **Variable overheads** are amounts of indirect cost that vary with the level of output or activity. As the level of output or activity rises then so does any variable overhead cost.

1.4 REASONS FOR ABSORPTION COSTING

The main reasons for wanting to calculate full costs, as indicated earlier, are mainly to value inventories of manufactured goods, and possibly also to calculate a selling price based on full costs.

Inventory valuation

The costs of making a product include the costs of direct materials, direct labour and direct expenses. In some organisations products are simply valued at this total figure for costing purposes. However the overheads incurred by the production departments are costs that are necessary to make those products. Production overheads, although indirect costs of the cost units, are as much a cost of the product as the direct costs.

Therefore in order to value closing inventory at the full cost of producing each product or cost unit, the cost unit incurred must include a share of the overheads in the product cost. The full cost of producing the product or cost unit is the total direct costs of the product plus its share of indirect production costs.

Pricing at a mark-up over full cost

One reason for costing products at their full cost could be for pricing purposes. If the price of a product is to cover all of the costs of the product plus some margin to give a profit then the full cost must be known in order to apply the profit margin. In the longer term, if absorption costing is used, a business will have a more informed idea of the long term profitability of a product as all production costs and revenues will have been considered.

Example

The cost of a unit of Product X is as follows:

	$
Direct materials	1.60
Direct labour	2.20
Direct expenses	0.40
Indirect expenses	0.80

If the organisation's policy is to cover all costs of a product and then make a profit equal to 20% of the total costs, at what price must Product X be sold?

Solution

Total cost of Product X

	$
Direct materials	1.60
Direct labour	2.20
Direct expenses	0.40
Indirect expenses	0.80
	5.00
Profit (20% × $5.00)	1.00
Selling price	6.00

2 TREATMENT OF OVERHEADS IN ABSORPTION COSTING

In absorption costing, products, services or activities are charged with a fair share of indirect costs. There is a three-stage process involved in charging overhead costs to products or services:

- overhead allocation

- overhead apportionment

- overhead absorption, also called overhead recovery.

Each of these stages is explained below. However, in order to appreciate overhead allocation and overhead apportionment, it is first of all necessary to know something about the type of cost centres found in manufacturing organisations.

2.1 COST CENTRES AND ABSORPTION COSTING

A business can decide what its cost centres should be. Generally-speaking, cost centres within a manufacturing organisation are likely to consist of:

- **Production departments**, in which items of product are manufactured. There could be several production departments within any organisation, and production might flow from one department to another and then another. For example, production might flow from a machining department to an assembly department and then a finishing department. Similarly, in textile production, work might flow from a carding department to a spinning department to a weaving department. Each production department might be a separate cost centre. Alternatively, a cost centre might be a single machine or a group of machines under the direction of one supervisor.

- **Service departments** within the production area. These are departments operating within the production function that are not involved directly in the manufacture of products. Instead, they provide service and support to production departments. These can include a stores department, a maintenance and repairs department, a production control department, and so on.

ABSORPTION COSTING : CHAPTER 8

- **Administration departments** or functions, for administration overheads.

- **Selling and distribution departments** or functions, for selling and distribution costs.

- **General cost items** that cannot be attributed to a single department or work area. Examples are rental costs for a factory building, lighting and heating costs, building security and maintenance costs, and so on.

In the description of absorption costing that follows, administration overheads and selling and distribution overheads are ignored, and the focus of attention is on full production costs. Costs centres will therefore be categorised as production departments, service departments and general costs.

3 OVERHEAD ALLOCATION

Overhead allocation is the first of the three stages in establishing a full cost for a product or service.

Definition **Overhead allocation** is the process of charging a whole item of cost to a cost centre.

ACTIVITY 1

A manufacturing business operates with two production departments, P and Q and a service department S. It manufactures widgets. It incurs the following costs in a given period.

	$
Labour costs in Department S	6,500
Direct labour costs in Department P	4,700
Costs of supervision in Department Q	2,100
Material costs of widgets	10,300
Machine repair costs, Department Q	800
Materials consumed in Department S	1,100
Depreciation of machinery in Department S	700
Indirect materials consumed in Department P	500
Lighting and heating	900
Costs of works canteen	1,500

Required:

Allocate these costs as overhead costs to the following cost centres:

    production Department P

    production Department Q

    service Department S

    a cost centre for general costs.

Indicate with reasons why you have not allocated any of the cost items in the list.

For a suggested answer, see the 'Answers' section at the end of the book.

KAPLAN PUBLISHING

4 APPORTIONMENT OF OVERHEAD COSTS

Once overhead costs have been allocated to cost centres, general overheads must be shared out, or apportioned. This may be to production or service cost centres.

Definition **Overhead apportionment** is the process of sharing out overhead costs on a fair basis.

Apportionment should be on a fair basis, but there are no rules about what 'fair' means.

An organisation should establish, for each item of general cost, what this basis ought to be. For many costs, there are two or more different bases that could be used.

Some examples should help to illustrate the considerations involved.

4.1 EXAMPLES

Example 1

A general cost in a manufacturing company is factory rental. Annual rental costs are $80,000. How should this cost be apportioned between production cost centres and service cost centres?

Rental costs are usually apportioned between cost centres on the basis of the floor space taken up by each cost centre. For example, suppose that three cost centres have floor space of 10,000 square metres, 15,000 square metres and 25,000 square metres, and annual rental costs are $80,000. If we apportion rental costs between the cost centres on the basis of their floor space, the apportionment would be as follows:

Annual rental	$80,000
Total floor space (10,000 + 15,000 + 25,000)	50,000 square metres
Apportionment rate ($80,000/50,000)	$1.60/square metre

	$
Apportion to cost centre with 10,000 square metres	16,000
Apportion to cost centre with 15,000 square metres	24,000
Apportion to cost centre with 25,000 square metres	40,000
	80,000

Example 2

The costs of heating and lighting might also be apportioned on the basis of floor space. Alternatively, since heating relates to volume rather than floor space, it could be argued that the costs should be apportioned on the volume of space taken up by each cost centre. Yet another view is that electricity costs relate more to the consumption of electrical power by machines, therefore the apportionment of these costs should be on the basis of the number and power of the machines in each cost centre.

A reasonable argument could be made for any of these bases of apportionment.

ABSORPTION COSTING : CHAPTER 8

Example 3

Supervisors' costs could be apportioned on either of the following bases:

- the number of employees in each cost centre

- the hours worked by employees in each department (on the grounds that the costs relate more to the number of hours in attendance at work rather than the numbers of employees).

ACTIVITY 2

What would be the most appropriate basis of apportionment of the following overheads?

(a) Oil used for machine lubrication.

(b) Depreciation of machinery.

(c) Petrol for vehicles used by the organisation.

For a suggested answer, see the 'Answers' section at the end of the book.

5 OVERHEAD ANALYSIS SHEET

A record of the overheads allocated and apportioned can be set out on an overhead analysis sheet.

5.1 OVERHEAD ANALYSIS SHEET: OVERHEAD APPORTIONMENT

The purpose of the analysis sheet is to show how the overhead costs are built up for each production and service cost centre.

5.2 WORKED EXAMPLE

The example below illustrates the apportionment of overheads using an overhead analysis sheet.

This example stops at the point where general overheads have been apportioned to production departments and service departments. It does not show how service departments are re-apportioned to the production departments.

Note that this example is longer than any question that could be asked for in an exam. But it should explain all the possible elements that you could be asked to calculate in this area.

MA 2 : MANAGING COSTS AND FINANCES

Example

An organisation has two production departments, A and B, and two service departments, stores and the canteen.

The overhead costs for the organisation in total are as follows:

	$
Rent	32,000
Building maintenance costs	5,000
Machinery insurance	2,400
Machinery depreciation	11,000
Machinery running expenses	6,000
Power	7,000

There are also specific costs that have already been allocated to each cost centre as follows:

	$
Department A	5,000
Department B	4,000
Stores	1,000
Canteen	2,000

The following information about the various cost centres is also available:

	Total	Dept A	Dept B	Stores	Canteen
Floor space (sq ft)	30,000	15,000	8,000	5,000	2,000
Power usage	100%	45%	40%	5%	10%
Value of machinery ($000)	250	140	110	–	–
Machinery hours (000)	80	50	30		
Value of equipment ($000)	20	–	–	5	15
Number of Employees	40	20	15	3	2
Value of stores Requisitions ($000)	150	100	50	–	–

Required:

Allocate and apportion the costs to the four departments.

Do not reapportion the service cost centre costs to the production cost centre.

5.3 SOLUTION

OVERHEAD ANALYSIS SHEET			PERIOD ENDING..................		
	TOTAL	PRODUCTION		SERVICE	
	$	Dept A $	Dept B $	Stores $	Canteen $
Overheads allocated directly to cost centres	12,000	5,000	4,000	1,000	2,000
Overheads to be apportioned					
Rent Basis: floor space 15/30 × $32,000 8/30 × $32,000 5/30 × $32,000 2/30 × $32,000	32,000	16,000	8,534	5,333	2,133
Building maintenance Basis: floor space 15/30 × $5,000 8/30 × $5,000 5/30 × $5,000 2/30 × $5,000	5,000	2,500	1,333	834	333
Machinery insurance Basis: machine value 140/250 × $2,400 110/250 × $2,400	2,400	1,344	1,056	–	–
Machinery depreciation Basis: machine value 140/250 × $11,000 110/250 × $11,000	11,000	6,160	4,840	–	–
Machinery running expenses Basis: machine hours 50/80 × $6,000 30/80 × $6,000	6,000	3,750	2,250	–	–
Power Basis: power usage percentages $7,000 × 45% $7,000 × 40% $7,000 × 5% $7,000 × 10%	7,000	3,150	2,800	350	700
Allocated and apportioned costs	75,400	37,904	24,813	7,517	5,166

6 SERVICE COST CENTRE RE-APPORTIONMENT

The aim of allocating and apportioning production overheads is to establish the total overhead costs for each production cost centre. In order to achieve this, the overhead costs that have been allocated and apportioned to service cost centres within production have to be re-apportioned to the production cost centres.

There are two main methods of service cost centre re-apportionment:

- Direct method – this method is used where service cost centres do not provide services for one another.

- Step-down method – this method is used where at least one of the service cost centres provides a service to another service cost centre as well as to the production cost centres.

When service cost centre overheads are re-apportioned, the end result is the same. All overhead costs are charged to production departments. However, the amount of overheads charged to each production department will be different. In other words, the direct method and the step-down method will share out the overhead costs in a different way.

6.1 DIRECT METHOD OF RE-APPORTIONMENT

With the direct method of re-apportionment, general overheads which have been apportioned to service cost centres will be re-apportioned to production cost centres only. The order of re-apportionment is irrelevant with this method.

Example – direct method of re-apportionment

Using the information produced in the previous worked example, the allocated and apportioned overhead costs are:

OVERHEAD ANALYSIS SHEET		PERIOD ENDING................			
	TOTAL	PRODUCTION		SERVICE	
		Dept A	Dept B	Stores	Canteen
	$	$	$	$	$
Total overhead	75,400	37,904	24,813	7,517	5,166

The apportionment of the stores department costs will be on the basis of the value of requisitions by each production cost centre. The apportionment of the canteen costs should be on the basis of the number of employees in production departments A and B.

It is assumed that the stores cost centre does no work for the canteen and the canteen does no work for the stores cost centre.

Consequently, none of the stores costs should be apportioned to the canteen and none of the canteen costs should be apportioned to stores.

The following data is available:

	Total	Dept A	Dept B	Stores	Canteen
Number of employees	40	20	15	3	2
Value of stores requisitions ($000)	150	100	50	–	–

Required:

Show how the service cost centre costs should be re-apportioned, and the resulting total overhead costs of each production cost centre.

Solution

OVERHEAD ANALYSIS SHEET			PERIOD ENDING..................		
	TOTAL	**PRODUCTION**		**SERVICE**	
		Dept A	Dept B	Stores	Canteen
	$	$	$	$	$
Allocated/apportioned overhead	75,400	37,904	24,813	7,517	5,166
Apportion stores Basis: requisitions 100/150 × $7,517 50/150 × $7,517		5,011	2,506	(7,517)	
Apportion canteen Basis: number of employees 20/35 × $5,166 15/35 × $5,166		2,952	2,214		(5,166)
Total overhead		45,867	29,533		

Conclusion This is the simplest situation, where the service cost centres are isolated from each other. The assumption is implicit that the stores personnel do not use the canteen and that the canteen does not use the stores function. This is a situation where service centres do not service each other.

6.2 STEP-DOWN METHOD OF RE-APPORTIONMENT

With the step-down method, a service cost centre's costs are first re-apportioned to production cost centres and another service cost centre. The second service cost centre's total cost, which now includes a share of the first service cost centre's cost, is re-apportioned to production cost centres. Unlike the direct method, the order of re-apportionment is relevant with the step-down method.

Example – step-down method of re-apportionment

Suppose that, in the previous example, stores cost centre employees use the canteen. The solution would now change as follows:

MA 2 : MANAGING COSTS AND FINANCES

Solution

OVERHEAD ANALYSIS SHEET			PERIOD ENDING...............		
	TOTAL	PRODUCTION		SERVICE	
		Dept A	Dept B	Stores	Canteen
	$	$	$	$	$
Allocated/apportioned overhead	75,400	37,904	24,813	7,517	5,166
Apportion canteen Basis: number of employees 20/38 × $5,166 15/38 × $5,166 3/38 × $5,166		2,719	2,039	408	(5,166)
Apportion stores Basis: requisitions 100/150 × $7,925 50/150 × $7,925		5,283	2,642	(7,925)	
Total overhead		45,906	29,494		

Note: The key to this step-down method of re-apportionment is to start by re-apportioning the overhead costs of the service cost centre that does work for the other service cost centre.

ACTIVITY 3

A manufacturing business has two production cost centres and two service cost centres. The allocated overhead costs and apportioned general overhead costs for each cost centre are as follows.

	$
Production cost centre P1	140,000
Production cost centre P2	200,000
Service cost centre S1	90,000
Service cost centre S2	120,000

Required:

(a) Show how the overheads would be charged to each production cost centre if it is assumed that neither service cost centre does any work for the other. Cost centre S1 does 60% of its work for P1 and 40% of its work for P2. Cost centre S2 does one-third of its work for P1 and two-thirds of its work for P2.

(b) Show how the overheads would be charged to each production cost centre if it is assumed that service cost centre S2 does work for cost centre S1 as well as the two production cost centres, as indicated in the table below.

	Apportionment ratio			
	Cost centre P1	Cost centre P2	Cost centre S1	Cost centre S2
Cost centre S1	60%	40%	–	–
Cost centre S2	25%	50%	25%	–

For a suggested answer, see the 'Answers' section at the end of the book.

ABSORPTION COSTING : CHAPTER 8

7 THE ARBITRARY NATURE OF OVERHEAD APPORTIONMENTS

At the end of the process of allocation and apportionment of production overheads, all overhead costs have been charged to production cost centres.

The process of apportionment attempts to be fair, but the selection of the bases for apportionment is based on judgement and assumption.

- General cost items can often be apportioned on any of two or more different bases, and depending on the basis chosen, the amount of cost charged to each responsibility centre/cost centre will differ.

- Similarly, the basis for apportioning service department costs to production departments can differ, depending on the assumptions made or point of view taken.

- The decision about whether to allow for the work done by service departments for other service departments is also significant. The assumption chosen will affect the amount of overheads charged from the service departments to each production department.

Methods of apportioning overheads should be kept under review, to make sure that they remain valid and sensible.

If a basis of apportionment no longer appears valid, a change in the apportionment basis should be proposed to management, giving the reasons for the proposed change.

8 OVERHEAD ABSORPTION

Allocation and apportionment are the first two stages in the process of charging overhead costs to products or services.

The third stage in the absorption costing process is overhead absorption, also called overhead recovery.

Definition   **Overhead absorption** is the process of adding overhead costs to the cost of a product or service, in order to build up a fully-absorbed product cost or service cost.

As a result of overhead absorption, in theory at least, the total amount of overheads incurred should be absorbed into the costs of the products manufactured (or services provided) by the business.

8.1 BASIS OF ABSORPTION

Production overhead costs are absorbed into product costs on a basis selected by the organisation. The absorption basis should be appropriate for the particular products or services. The most common bases of absorption are:

- an absorption rate per unit, but only if the organisation produces a single product or several standard products

- an absorption rate per direct labour hour worked

MA 2 : MANAGING COSTS AND FINANCES

- an absorption rate per machine hour worked
- an absorption rate based on a percentage of direct labour costs
- an absorption rate based on a percentage of prime cost (a percentage of direct materials, direct labour and direct expense costs).

The only bases for absorption required for your syllabus are direct labour hours and machine hours.

8.2 ABSORPTION RATES

An absorption rate is the rate at which overheads are added to costs.

- If the absorption basis is direct labour hours worked, the absorption rate will be $Y per direct labour hour. For example, if the absorption rate for production overhead is $5 per direct labour hour, a job taking 4 direct labour hours will be charged with $20 of overhead.

- If the absorption basis is machine hours worked, the absorption rate will be $Z per machine hour. For example, if the absorption rate for production overhead is $15 per machine hour, a job taking 2 machine hours will be charged with $30 of overhead.

The absorption rate is calculated as:

$$\frac{\text{Overhead costs}}{\text{Volume of activity (direct labour hours, machine hours)}}$$

Overhead costs for any production department are the allocated and apportioned overheads, assembled by the methods described above.

An organisation might have just one absorption rate for its entire production operations. However, an organisation with more than one production department is likely to have a different absorption rate for each department, so that separately-calculated production overheads are added to product costs for the work done in each department.

The basis of absorption can differ between production departments and the absorption rate can differ between departments.

8.3 ABSORPTION RATES BASED ON THE BUDGET

It might seem logical that overhead absorption rates should be based on the actual overhead costs in a period and the actual volume of activity (direct labour hours or machine hours worked, or units produced).

In practice, this is not the case. Overhead absorption rates are based on budgeted overhead costs and the budgeted volume of activity.

$$\text{Absorption rate} = \frac{\text{Budgeted overhead costs}}{\text{Budgeted volume of activity}}$$

There are several important reasons for using budgeted figures:

1	If we used actual costs we would have to wait until after the end of the period to calculate product costs. This is because actual overhead costs cannot be known until the period has ended and information about actual costs has been gathered and analysed.

2	As full product cost is often used as a basis to set prices, it needs to be known in advance.

3	Overheads, by their nature, are often incurred unevenly throughout the year. For example, heating costs may be higher in the winter, holiday pay may be higher in the summer. By using budgeted costs to calculate an absorption rate, overheads can be spread fairly to all production units throughout the year.

4	The 'average' cost calculated should recover all overhead costs and provides a stable basis to establish prices.

By using absorption rates based on budgeted overhead spending and budgeted activity volume, we can establish absorption rates in advance, and charge overhead costs to products as soon as they are made (and to services as soon as they are performed).

8.4 OVERHEAD ABSORPTION

Once an overhead absorption rate has been calculated, the amount of overhead absorbed can be calculated as follows:

Overhead absorbed = Actual activity level × Budgeted overhead absorption rate

For example, if the budgeted overhead absorption rate of Department M is $8 per machine hour, and the actual machine hours worked in Period 1 were 1,700, the overhead absorbed would be:

Overhead absorbed (Department M) = 1,700 machine hours × $8 = $13,600

The following example shows how the overheads absorbed by three different departments are incorporated into the cost of a job.

Example

Job 1234 goes through three production departments. The direct materials cost of the job are $200 and the direct labour costs are:

Department 1	(3 direct labour hours)	$18
Department 2	(1.5 direct labour hours)	$12
Department 3	(6 direct labour hours)	$48

The job takes 3 machine hours in department 2.

The production overhead absorption rates are:

Department 1	$5 per direct labour hour
Department 2	$10 per machine hour
Department 3	$12 per direct labour hour

Required:

Calculate the full production cost of Job 1234.

Solution

		$	$
Direct materials			200
Direct labour:			
Department 1		18	
Department 2		12	
Department 3		48	
			78
Production overhead:			
Department 1	(3 direct labour hours at $5 per hour)	15	
Department 2	(3 machine hours at $10 per hour)	30	
Department 3	(6 direct labour hours at $12 per hour)	72	
			117
Full cost of the job			395

ACTIVITY 4

Cuecraft Ltd manufactures pool and snooker cues. It has three production cost centres:

- machining
- finishing
- packing.

The planned overhead for the next budget period has been allocated and apportioned to the cost centres as:

Machining	$65,525
Finishing	$36,667
Packing	$24,367

Budgeted cost centre activity volumes for the same period show:

Machining	7,300 machine hours
Finishing	6,250 direct labour hours
Packing	5,200 direct labour hours

Required:

Determine separate overhead absorption (recovery) rates for each cost centre on the following bases:

- Machining – machine hours
- Finishing – direct labour hours
- Packing – direct labour hours.

For a suggested answer, see the 'Answers' section at the end of the book.

ACTIVITY 5

Assume that Cuecraft produces a pool cue 'pot 3' and it takes 4 hours to complete.

The activity takes place in the following cost centres:

Machining   3 hrs

Finishing   0.9 hr

Packing   0.1 hr

Using the overhead absorption rates calculated in Activity 4, show the overhead recovered in a unit of 'pot 3'.

For a suggested answer, see the 'Answers' section at the end of the book.

9   UNDER- AND OVER-ABSORPTION OF OVERHEADS

Overhead absorption rates are based on budgeted overhead costs and the budgeted volume of activity; they are pre-determined.

In practice, for each accounting period, it is often the case that:

- actual overhead expenditure will differ from budgeted overhead expenditure, and

- the actual volume of activity will differ from the budgeted volume of activity.

As a consequence, the amount of overheads charged to product costs will differ from the actual overhead expenditure.

We might charge more overhead costs to production than the amount of overhead expenditure actually incurred. If so, there is over-absorbed or over-recovered overheads.

We might charge less in overhead costs to production than the amount of overhead expenditure actually incurred. If so, there is under-absorbed or under-recovered overheads.

Over-absorbed overhead during a period is treated as an addition to profit, because it is an adjustment to allow for the fact that too much overhead cost has been charged to the items produced in the period. Similarly, under-absorbed overhead during a period is treated as a reduction in profit, because it is an adjustment to allow for the fact that the overhead cost charged to the items produced in the period is less than the actual overhead costs incurred.

Example

A company has a single production department. Its budgeted production overheads for 20X4 were $200,000 and its budgeted volume of production was 50,000 direct labour hours. The company has decided to absorb production overheads into product costs on a direct labour hour basis.

During 20X4, actual production overhead expenditure was $195,000 and 54,000 direct labour hours were worked.

The absorption rate is $4 per direct labour hour ($200,000/50,000 hours, based on the budget).

MA 2 : MANAGING COSTS AND FINANCES

The overheads absorbed into product costs are $4 for each direct labour hour actually worked.

	$
Total production overheads absorbed (54,000 hours × $4)	216,000
Overheads actually incurred	195,000
Over-absorbed overheads	21,000

Here, overheads are over-absorbed because $216,000 in production overhead costs has been charged to the cost of items produced, but actual overhead spending was only $195,000. Production has been charged with too much overhead.

Over-absorbed overhead is taken to the income statement as an addition to profit in the period, to compensate for the fact that the recorded costs of production are in excess of actual expenditure.

Example

For the year ended 31 December 20X4 the planned overhead for the Machining Cost Centre at Cuecraft Ltd was:

Overhead	$132,000
Volume of activity	15,000 machine hours

In January 20X4 the cost centre incurred $12,000 of overhead and 1,350 machine hours were worked.

Required:

Calculate the pre-determined overhead rate per machine hour and the overhead under or over-recovered in the month.

Solution

Absorption rate, based on the budget:

$$\frac{\text{Planned overhead}}{\text{Machine hours}} = \frac{\$132,000}{15,000 \text{ machine hours}} = \$8.80 \text{ per machine hour}$$

	$
Overhead absorbed	
1,350 machine hours at $8.80	11,880
Overhead incurred	12,000
Under-absorbed overhead	120

Here, the amount of overheads actually charged to production are $11,880, which is less than actual expenditure. We therefore have under absorption of overhead.

Under recovery of overheads is shown as a separate item in the costing income statement. Since production has been charged with less overheads than the amount of overheads incurred, under absorption is shown as a cost in the income statement, thereby reducing the profit.

ABSORPTION COSTING : CHAPTER 8

ACTIVITY 6

A manufacturing business has two production departments, X and Y, for which the following annual budgeted figures have been prepared.

	Department X	Department Y
Budgeted overhead expenditure	$840,000	$720,000
Overhead absorption basis	Machine hours	Direct labour hours
Budgeted activity	40,000 machine hours	60,000 direct labour hours

Actual overhead expenditure and actual activity levels for the year were:

	Department X	Department Y
Actual overhead expenditure	$895,000	$735,000
Actual activity	41,500 machine hours	62,400 direct labour hours

Required:

(a) Establish the overhead absorption rates for each department for the year.

(b) Calculate the under- or over-absorbed overhead in each department for the year.

For a suggested answer, see the 'Answers' section at the end of the book.

10 ACCOUNTING FOR PRODUCTION OVERHEADS

If a manufacturing business maintains cost accounts in a cost ledger, overheads are accounted for within the double entry bookkeeping system of the cost ledger.

Three accounts are particularly relevant to accounting for production overheads:

- the **production overhead account.** This account is debited with the actual cost of indirect materials, labour and expenses and credited with overhead absorbed to production. The balance on this account represents over- or under-absorbed overhead and is either written off directly to the income statement or is passed to an under/over-absorbed overhead account

- the **work-in-progress account.** This account is debited with production overhead absorbed. The full cost of production is therefore built up on the debit side of this account

- the **under- or over-absorbed overhead account.** This account collects under/over absorption balances from the production overhead account prior to write off to the income statement.

KAPLAN PUBLISHING   145

The entries in these accounts are as follows:

Production overheads account

Debit side (overheads incurred)	$	Credit side (overheads absorbed)	$
Stores account (indirect materials)	X	Work-in-progress account (overheads absorbed)	X
Wages control account (indirect labour)	X		
Various accounts (indirect expenses)	X		
[Over-absorbed overhead] (balancing figure)	X	[Under-absorbed overhead] (balancing figure)	X
	X		X

Work-in-progress account

Debit side (elements of production cost)	$	Credit side (completed production)	$
Opening inventory, work-in-progress			
Stores account (direct materials)	X	Finished goods account (completed production)	X
Wages control account (direct labour)	X		
Production overhead account (production overhead absorbed)	X	Closing inventory, work-in-progress	X
	X		X

If under-absorbed

Under-/over-absorbed overhead account

Debit side	$	Credit side	$
Production overhead account	X	Income statement	X
	X		X

If over-absorbed

Under-/over-absorbed overhead account

Debit side	$	Credit side	$
Income statement	X	Production overhead account	X
	X		X

Example

A manufacturing business has a single production department. It uses absorption costing and absorbs production overhead into costs on a direct labour hour basis.

The production overhead budget for the year to 30 June 20X4 was $800,000, and budgeted direct labour hours were 100,000.

During the year to 30 June 20X4, the following costs were incurred:

	$
Direct materials	420,000
Indirect materials	40,000
Direct labour	750,000
Indirect labour	315,000
Indirect expenses	505,000

Opening work-in-progress was $90,000 and closing work-in-progress was $70,000.

The number of labour hours actually worked was 110,000 hours.

Required:

Prepare the following accounts in the cost ledger of the business.

- Production overhead account
- Work-in-progress account
- Under-/over-absorbed overhead account.

Solution

Workings

The overhead absorption rate is $8 per direct labour hour ($800,000/100,000 hours).

Production overheads absorbed were $880,000 (110,000 hours × $8 per hour).

Production overheads account

	$		$
Stores account	40,000	Work-in-progress	880,000
Wages control account	315,000		
Indirect expenses	505,000		
Over-absorbed overhead	20,000		
	880,000		880,000

Work-in-progress account

	$		$
Opening inventory	90,000	Finished goods	2,070,000
Stores	420,000	(balancing figure)	
Wages control	750,000		
Production overhead	880,000	Closing inventory	70,000
	2,140,000		2,140,000

Under-/over-absorbed overhead account

	$		$
Income statement	20,000	Production overhead account	20,000
	20,000		20,000

11 INVESTIGATING THE CAUSES OF UNDER- OR OVER-ABSORBED OVERHEAD

The intention of absorbing production overhead is to share the costs of the overheads among the various products manufactured or jobs worked on. Ideally, the amount of over-head absorbed should equal the amount of overhead expenditure incurred. In practice, this rarely happens, and there are some under- or over-absorbed overheads. This is because the absorption rate is decided in advance, based on the budgeted overhead expenditure and budgeted volume of activity.

Even so, the amount of under- or over-absorbed overhead should not usually be large, provided the budgeting is realistic and provided that actual results meet budgeted expectations.

If the amount of under- or over-absorbed overhead is large, something could have gone wrong, which should be a matter of some concern to management. Certainly, management should expect to be informed of the reasons why there has been a large amount of under- or over-absorption.

The accountant will be expected to investigate the reasons for the under- or over-absorption, and report his or her findings to management.

There are several reasons why a large amount of under or over absorption of overhead might occur.

- Actual overhead expenditure was much higher than budgeted, possibly due to poor control over overhead spending.

- Actual overhead expenditure was much less than budgeted, possibly due to good control over overhead spending.

- Actual overhead expenditure was much higher or lower than budgeted, due to poor budgeting of overhead expenditure.

- The actual volume of activity was higher or lower than budgeted, for operational reasons that the production manager should be able to explain.

- The actual volume of activity was higher or lower than budgeted, due to poor budgeting of the volume of activity.

12 NON-PRODUCTION OVERHEADS

In a system of absorption costing, it is quite usual for administration overheads and sales and distribution overheads to be treated as period costs and written as a charge to the income statement, instead of being added to the cost of cost units.

However, it is also possible to calculate a full cost of sale by absorbing non-production overheads into costs.

- Administration overheads might be absorbed into unit costs as a percentage of full production cost.

- Sales and distribution overheads might be absorbed into unit costs as either a percentage of sales value, or as a percentage of full production cost.

Example

Sleepy Limited has budgeted the following sales and costs for next year.

	$
Full production costs	240,000
Administration overheads	60,000
Sales and distribution overheads	80,000
Sales revenue	450,000

Production overheads will be absorbed at the rate of $4 per direct labour hour. Administration overheads will be absorbed as a percentage of full production cost. Sales and distribution overhead will also be absorbed as a percentage of full production cost.

Required:

Calculate the fully absorbed cost of sale for a product that has a direct material cost of $240 and a direct labour cost of $160, with labour paid at the rate of $8 per hour.

Solution

Administration overheads will be absorbed at the rate of 25% (60,000/240,000) of full production cost.

Sales and distribution overheads will be absorbed at the rate of 33.33% (80,000/240,000) of full production cost.

The full cost of sale for the product is:

	$
Direct materials	240
Direct labour	160
Production overheads (20 hours × $4)	80
Full production cost	480
Administration overheads (25% × $480)	120
Sales and distribution overheads (33.33% × $480)	160
Full cost of sale	760

MA 2 : MANAGING COSTS AND FINANCES

13 FIXED, VARIABLE AND SEMI-FIXED OVERHEADS

In the examples above, overheads have been treated as a total cost. An organisation might, however, distinguish between its fixed overheads and variable overheads, and apply a different overhead absorption rate for each.

To do this, it might be necessary in the budget to separate semi-fixed and semi-variable overhead costs into their fixed and variable elements.

This can be done using the high-low method, which we met in Chapter 3.

Example

It has been estimated that total production overhead costs are as follows:

	$
At 16,000 direct labour hours of work	86,000
At 19,000 direct labour hours of work	89,750

Required:

(a) Use these estimates to obtain a fixed overhead absorption rate and a variable overhead absorption rate for the budget period, in which the budgeted level of activity is 18,000 direct labour hours. Both the fixed overhead and variable overhead absorption rate should be on a direct labour hour basis.

(b) Suppose that actual results during the period were as follows:

Total overheads incurred	$90,600
Direct labour hours worked	17,400

Calculate the amount of under- or over-absorbed overhead.

Solution

(a)

		$
At 19,000 hours	the cost is	89,750
At 16,000 hours	the cost is	86,000
The difference is	3,000 hours	and 3,750

The difference must represent variable cost as by definition fixed costs do not change with activity.

Variable overhead cost per hour is therefore
($3,750/3,000) $1.25

This is the absorption rate for variable overheads.

	$
As total overhead cost of 19,000 hours is	89,750
And total variable overhead cost of 19,000 hours (× $1.25) is	23,750
Therefore fixed costs must be	66,000

The absorption rate for fixed overhead, given a budget of 18,000 direct labour hours, should therefore be $3.667 per direct labour hour.

(b)

	$
Absorbed overheads:	
Fixed (17,400 hours × $3.67)	63,858
Variable (17,400 × $1.25)	21,750
Total absorbed overheads	85,608
Overheads incurred	90,600
Under-absorbed overhead	4,992

ACTIVITY 7

A manufacturing business uses absorption costing, and establishes separate absorption rates for fixed production overhead and variable production overhead. The absorption rates for next year will be based on 40,000 direct labour hours. Expenditure budgets for fixed and variable costs should be derived from the following estimates of cost:

	$
At 37,000 direct labour hours of work	145,500
At 42,000 direct labour hours of work	153,000

Actual results for the period were:

Direct labour hours worked	41,500 hours
Variable overhead costs incurred	$67,500
Fixed overhead costs incurred	$91,000

Required:

(a) Establish a fixed overhead absorption rate and a variable overhead absorption rate for the year.

(b) Calculate the amount of under- or over-absorbed overhead for both fixed and variable overhead.

(c) Prepare the following accounts for the cost ledger:

- production overhead account

- under- /over-absorbed overhead account.

For a suggested answer, see the 'Answers' section at the end of the book.

ACTIVITY 8

For the year ended 31 December 20X4 the planned overhead for finishing and packing cost centres at Cuecraft Ltd was $74,000 and $49,000 and cost centre activity volumes were planned as 12,750 and 10,500 direct labour hours.

During January 20X4 the following information was available:

	Finishing	Packing
Overhead incurred	$6,900	$4,000
Activity		
Direct labour hours	1,100	900

Calculate the pre-determined overhead recovery rates and the overhead under or over-recovered for each cost centre for the month, showing clearly the entries in the overhead control account.

For a suggested answer, see the 'Answers' section at the end of the book.

CONCLUSION

Absorption costing is a very important and complex topic. This chapter explained how to build up a full product cost by including an absorbed amount of overhead. This involved allocation, apportionment and absorption of overhead. You should also be prepared to calculate under or over absorption of overheads and carry out bookkeeping entries in relation to overheads.

KEY TERMS

Overheads – a term for indirect costs.

Absorption costing – a method of costing in which the costs of an item (product or service or activity) are built up as the sum of direct costs and a fair share of overhead costs, to obtain a full cost or a fully-absorbed cost.

Overhead allocation – the process of charging a whole item of cost to a cost centre.

Overhead apportionment – the process of sharing out overhead costs on a fair basis.

Overhead absorption – the process of adding overhead costs to the cost of a product or service, in order to build up a fully-absorbed product cost or service cost.

Under-absorption – overhead absorbed into the product is less than overhead incurred. Under absorption reduces calculated profit.

Over-absorption – overhead absorbed into the product is greater than overhead incurred. Over absorption increases calculated profit.

High-low method – a technique used to separate fixed and variable costs.

ABSORPTION COSTING : CHAPTER 8

SELF TEST QUESTIONS

		Paragraph
1	What are the reasons for using absorption costing?	1.4
2	What are service cost centres?	2.1
3	What bases of apportionment are used for overheads?	4
4	What is the difference between the direct and step-down method of overhead reapportionment?	6
5	What are the particular problems of dealing with service cost centres?	6
6	What are the common methods of absorbing overhead?	8.1
7	Why are absorption rates based on budgeted figures?	8.3
8	What is over and under recovery of overhead?	9
9	What is the accounting entry for production overhead absorbed?	11
10	What are the causes of under- or over-absorbed overhead?	12

EXAM-STYLE QUESTIONS

1 The process of cost apportionment is carried out so that:

   A   costs may be controlled

   B   cost units gather overheads as they pass through cost centres

   C   whole items of cost can be charged to cost centres

   D   common costs are shared among cost centres

2 What is cost allocation?

   A   The charging of discrete identifiable items of cost to cost centres

   B   The collection of costs attributable to cost centres and cost units using the costing methods, principles and techniques prescribed for a particular business entity

   C   The process of establishing the costs of cost centres or cost units

   D   The division of costs amongst two or more cost centres in proportion to the estimated benefit received, using a proxy e.g. square feet

KAPLAN PUBLISHING   153

3   A company absorbs overheads on the basis of machine hours which were budgeted at 11,250 with overheads of $258,750. Actual results were 10,980 hours with overheads of $254,692.

Overheads were:

A   under absorbed by $2,152

B   over absorbed by $4,058

C   under absorbed by $4,058

D   over absorbed by $2,152

4   The following budgeted and actual data relate to production activity and overhead costs in Winnie Ltd.

	Budget	Actual
Production overhead		
Fixed	$94,000	$102,600
Variable	$57,500	$62,000
Direct labour hours	25,000	26,500

The company uses an absorption costing system and production overheads are absorbed on a direct labour hour basis.

Production overhead during the period was:

A   under absorbed by $4,010

B   over absorbed by $4,010

C   under absorbed by $9,876

D   over absorbed by $9,876

5   An overhead absorption rate is used to:

A   share out common costs over benefiting cost centres

B   find the total overheads for a cost centre

C   charge overheads to products

D   control overheads

ABSORPTION COSTING : CHAPTER 8

6   Floaters plc has the following production and fixed overhead budgets for the coming year:

Production department	1	2
Fixed overhead	$2,400,000	$4,000,000
Total labour hours	240,000	200,000
Total materials cost	$200,000	$400,000

Department 1 labour is paid $5 per hour and department 2 labour $4 per hour.

The variable production cost of an IC is as follows:

			$
Labour			
Department 1	3 hours		15
Department 2	2 hours		8
Materials			
Department 1: 1 kg	@ $4 per kg		4
Department 2: 2 kgs	@ $5 per kg		10
Variable overheads			7
			$44

If fixed overheads are absorbed on the basis of labour hours, the fixed overhead cost per unit of IC is:

A $70

B $72.72

C $102.67

D $148

7   A company has four production departments. The following information is available:

Department	K	L	M	N
Fixed costs	$10,000	$5,000	$4,000	$6,000
Labour hours per unit	5	5	4	3

If the company recovers overheads on the basis of labour hours and plans to produce 2,000 units, then the fixed cost per unit is:

A $3.00

B $12.00

C $12.50

D $17.00

KAPLAN PUBLISHING

MA 2 : MANAGING COSTS AND FINANCES

8   A firm absorbs overheads on the basis of labour hours. In one period 11,500 hours were worked, actual overheads were $138,000 and there was $23,000 over absorption. The overhead absorption rate per hour was:

   A $10

   B $12

   C $13

   D $14

9   What will result if the budgeted level of activity is below the actual volume of activity and actual expenditure on fixed production overheads is the same as budget?

   A   There will be too much expenditure on fixed production overheads

   B   There will be too little expenditure on fixed production overheads

   C   Fixed production overheads will be over-absorbed

   D   Fixed production overheads will be under-absorbed

For a suggested answer, see the 'Answers' section at the end of the book.

Chapter 9

MARGINAL COSTING AND ABSORPTION COSTING

In the previous chapter, we looked at how absorption costing can be used to calculate the full cost of a cost unit, and how absorption costing can be used within a cost accounting double entry bookkeeping system. Absorption costing is not the only method of costing to measure costs and profits. An alternative costing method is marginal costing.

This chapter describes marginal costing and compares the marginal costing and absorption costing methods. This chapter covers syllabus area C2.

CONTENTS

1. Full cost and marginal cost
2. Contribution
3. Profit statements under absorption and marginal costing
4. Advantages of marginal costing
5. Advantages of absorption costing

LEARNING OUTCOMES

At the end of this chapter you should be able to:

- explain and illustrate the concept of contribution

- prepare profit statements using the marginal costing method

- compare and contrast the use of absorption and marginal costing for period profit reporting and inventory valuation

- reconcile the profits reported by absorption and marginal costing

- explain the usefulness of profit and contribution information respectively.

MA 2 : MANAGING COSTS AND FINANCES

1 FULL COST AND MARGINAL COST

In **absorption costing** fixed manufacturing overheads are absorbed into cost units. Thus, inventory is valued at total production cost and fixed manufacturing overheads are charged in the income statement of the period in which the units are sold.

In **marginal costing**, fixed manufacturing overheads are not absorbed into cost units. Inventory is valued at marginal or variable production cost. All fixed overheads, including fixed manufacturing overheads, are treated as period costs and are charged in the income statement of the period in which the overheads are incurred.

Example

Company A produces a single product and has the following budget:

Company A Budget per unit

	$
Selling price	10
Direct materials	3
Direct wages	2
Variable production overhead	1

Fixed production overhead is $10,000 per month; production volume is 5,000 units per month.

Calculate the cost per unit to be used for inventory valuation under:

(a) absorption costing

(b) marginal costing.

Solution

(a) **Full absorption cost per unit**

	$
Direct materials	3
Direct wages	2
Variable production overhead	1
Absorbed fixed production overhead $\dfrac{\$10,000}{5,000 \text{ units}}$	2
Full production cost per unit	$8

(b) **Marginal cost per unit**

	$
Direct materials	3
Direct wages	2
Variable production overhead	1
Marginal production cost per unit	$6

The **inventory valuation** will be different for marginal and absorption costing. Under absorption costing the inventory value will include variable and fixed production overheads whereas under marginal costing the inventory value will only include variable production overheads.

2 CONTRIBUTION

Contribution is an important concept in marginal costing. It is the difference between sales and the variable cost of sales. This can be written as:

Contribution = Sales – total variable cost of sales

Contribution is short for 'contribution to fixed costs and profits'. The idea is that after deducting the variable costs from sales, the figure remaining is the amount that contributes to fixed costs, and, once fixed costs are covered, to profits.

2.1 CONTRIBUTION AND PROFIT

Marginal costing values goods at variable cost of production (or marginal cost) and contribution can be shown as follows:

Marginal costing

	$
Sales	X
Less: all variable costs	(X)
Contribution	X
Less: fixed production costs	X
Less: all other fixed costs	X
Net profit	X

Profit is contribution less all fixed costs.

Note that there may be variable non-production costs which must also be deducted from sales to arrive at contribution.

In absorption costing profit is effectively calculated in one stage as the cost of sales already includes all overheads.

Absorption costing: profit calculation

	$
Sales	X
Less: absorption cost	(X)
Gross profit	X
Less: non-production costs	(X)
Net profit	X

2.2 WHY IS CONTRIBUTION SIGNIFICANT?

Contribution is an important concept in marginal costing. Changes in the volume of sales, or in sales prices, or in variable costs will all affect profit by altering the total contribution. Marginal costing techniques can be used to help management to assess the likely effect on profits of higher or lower sales volume, or the likely consequences of reducing the sales price of a product in order to increase demand, and so on. The approach to any such analysis should be to calculate the effect on total contribution. The arithmetic is quite straightforward.

MA 2 : MANAGING COSTS AND FINANCES

Example

A company sells a single product for $9. Its variable cost is $4. Fixed costs are currently $70,000 per annum and annual sales are 20,000 units. There is a proposal to make a change to the product design that would increase the variable cost to $4.50, but it would also be possible to increase the selling price to $10 for the re-designed model. It is expected that annual sales at this higher price would be 19,000 units.

How would the re-design of the product affect annual profit?

Solution

Annual profit is increased by $4,500 as a result of the proposal as follows:

	Before		After	
		$		$
Sales	(20,000 × $9)	180,000	(19,000 × $10)	190,000
Variable costs	(20,000 × $4)	80,000	(19,000 × $4.50)	85,500
Contribution		100,000		104,500
Fixed costs		70,000		70,000
Profit		30,000		34,500

An alternative presentation of the profit calculation is as follows:

	Before			After	
	Per unit ($)	$		Per unit	$
Sales	9			10	
Variable costs	4			4.50	
Contribution	5 × 20,000	100,000		5.50 × 19,000	104,500
Fixed costs		70,000			70,000
Profit		30,000			34,500

When calculating the impact of changes to sales price, variable cost and sales volume it is often quicker to calculate unit contribution figures. This approach also focuses on the key information which is important to managers when making a decision.

3 PROFIT STATEMENTS UNDER ABSORPTION AND MARGINAL COSTING

Absorption costing must be used to provide inventory valuations for statutory financial statements. However, either marginal or absorption costing can be useful for internal management reporting. The choice made will affect:

- the way in which the profit information is presented, and
- the level of reported profit, but only if sales volumes do not exactly equal production volumes (so that there is a difference between opening and closing inventory values).

Example

This example continues with the earlier example of Company A in Section 1.

Show profit statements for the month if sales are 4,800 units and production is 5,000 units under:

(a) absorption costing

(b) marginal costing.

Solution

(a) Profit statement under absorption costing

	$	$
Sales (4,800 at $10)		48,000
Less:		
Cost of sales		
Opening inventory	–	
Production (5,000 at $8)	40,000	
Less: Closing inventory (200 at $8)	(1,600)	
		(38,400)
Gross profit		$9,600

(b) Profit statement under marginal costing

	$	$
Sales (4,800 at $10)		48,000
Less:		
Cost of sales		
Opening inventory	–	
Production (5,000 at $6)	30,000	
Less: Closing inventory (200 at $6)	(1,200)	
		(28,800)
Contribution		19,200
Less: Fixed overheads		10,000
Gross profit		$9,200

Note that these profit statements only include production costs at this stage. A full profit statement is shown later in the chapter.

3.1 EXPLANATION OF THE DIFFERENCE IN PROFIT

The difference in profit between the two costing methods is due to the difference in inventory levels between the beginning and the end of the period. Here, there was an increase from 0 to 200 units during the month. Under absorption costing closing inventory has been valued at $1,600 (i.e. $8 per unit which includes $2 of absorbed fixed overheads). Under marginal costing closing inventory is valued at $1,200 (i.e. at $6 per unit) and all fixed overheads are charged to the income statement as a period cost.

If inventory levels are rising or falling, absorption costing will give a different profit figure from marginal costing. If sales equal production, the fixed overheads absorbed into cost of sales under absorption costing will be the same as the period costs charged under marginal costing and thus the profit figure will be the same.

The two profit figures can therefore be reconciled as follows:

	$
Absorption costing profit	9,600
Less: fixed costs included in the increase in inventory (200 × $2)	(400)
Marginal costing profit	9,200

MA 2 : MANAGING COSTS AND FINANCES

The basic rule

- If inventory levels are rising, AC profit > MC profit.
- If inventory levels are falling AC profit < MC profit.
- If opening and closing inventory levels are the same, AC profit = MC profit.

3.2 UNDER AND OVER ABSORPTION OF FIXED OVERHEADS

Under and over absorption of fixed overheads arises if the actual expenditure and production level are not as estimated in the predetermined overhead absorption rate. Such differences between budgeted and actual expenditure and production cause under or over absorption but have no effect on the different profit figures reported under absorption and marginal costing, which is due to the different inventory valuations. The next example illustrates this.

Example

A manufacturing business makes and sells widgets. It has 2,000 units in inventory at the start of the year. Budgeted production and sales for the year are 20,000 units. The variable production cost per unit is $6 and budgeted fixed costs are $80,000. The sales price per unit is $15. Ignore administration and selling and distribution overheads.

During the year, actual production and sales totalled 16,000 units. Unit variable costs and selling prices were as budgeted, and fixed costs were $77,000.

Required:

Compare the reported profit for the year with absorption costing and marginal costing.

Solution

Marginal costing

	$
Sales (16,000 × $15)	240,000
Variable cost of sales (16,000 × $6)	96,000
Contribution	144,000
Fixed costs	77,000
Profit	67,000

With absorption costing, the absorption rate is ($80,000/20,000) $4 per unit. So production and inventory is valued at $6 + $4 = $10.